Advance Praise

How important are relationships?
How important is Jill Avery's work?
How important is this book?

According to Derek Thompson *(The Atlantic*, February 2025), this is the anti-social century. "Socially underdeveloped childhood leads, almost inexorably, to socially stunted adulthood."

These are consequences not only for families but for the nation. It begins with the family.

—Dr. Barry Weston Hayes, PH.D
Clinical psychologist and
retired professor from Santa Clara University

PARENTS, GROW UP!

PARENTS, GROW UP!

Stop Wishing, Start Doing
Timeless Tools to Strengthen Your Family's Foundation and Relationships

Jill Avery

Parents, Grow Up: Stop Wishing, Start Doing, Timeless Tools to Strengthen Your Family's Foundation and Relationships
© Copyright 2025
Jill Avery

All rights reserved.

No part of this publication may be reproduced, distributed, or transmitted in any form or by any means, electronic or mechanical, including photocopying, recording, or by any information storage and retrieval system without the prior written permission of the author, except for the inclusion of brief quotations in critical reviews and certain other noncommercial uses permitted by copyright law. For permission, please contact the author.

DISCLAIMER
The content of this book is provided for informational and inspirational purposes only and is based on my life experiences and insights gained from empowering others. It is not a substitute for professional advice, diagnosis, or treatment. While the material may touch on topics related to wellness, mental health, or family dynamics, it is not intended to serve as therapy or counseling. For any concerns related to mental health or therapeutic needs, always consult a qualified professional.

Ebook: 978-1964014555
Softcover: 978-1964014562
Hardback: 978-1964014579

Library of Congress Control Number: 2025902732.

Cover Design via Made by Izzy
Published by Tasfil Publishing, LLC
Voorhees, New Jersey

It's a Family Affair

Mom: My whole life, I've seen, heard, and felt your love.

Poppy: You are with me. Every. Single. Moment.

Tanner and Autumn: I will always love you too much. Deal with it!

Charley: Your humor—a national treasure for our family.

*My Army Ranger: You always believed I could.
Thank you, Torpedo Boy.*

Zu: King of family fun and making memories—with snacks in hand.

Kathleen Jacoby: I hear your voice, still.

Cleo and Pistol: My nocturnal companions.

Lottie: Beside me always. I couldn't have done this without you.

Contents

Foreword 1
Introduction 3
Chapter 1: Getting Real, Real Quick 13
Chapter 2: The Magnificent 8 31
Chapter 3: Understanding the Young Brain 45
Chapter 4: In Family, We Trust 57
Chapter 5: Mindset Shifts for Mastering Your Response + Abilities 65
Chapter 6: Tools for Conversations, Connection, and Understanding 85
Chapter 7: Be the Muse 97
Chapter 8: The Muse Method: Family Activities that Bond and Brighten 115
Chapter 9: Grab Bag Goodies! 127
Conclusion: Yes, You're Ready! 153
It Matters 163
Acknowledgments 165
About the Author 169
Index 171

Foreword

First and foremost, as Jill's children, we are so proud to have the unique honor of writing the foreword for her book. Throughout her journey as a family empowerment coach, we have seen the profound difference she has made in the many families she has worked with. But even more special than that, we have reaped the benefits of her not only talking the talk but also walking the walk within our own family system. The tools that our mom details in this book are not just some flowery words between two covers. They are how she, herself, leads as a parent, and we, as her children, passionately endorse her mission.

Let's be real here: there is *no* such thing as a perfect parent, our mom included. As she would be the first to tell you, parenting is not always smooth sailing. Just because you're a parent doesn't mean you've finished growing up! In fact, the stages of parenthood might test you and your growth more than any other endeavor. But where our mom has done an exceptional job as a parent is by taking the tough moments in stride with the good and learning not only from her clients' experiences but also from her own mistakes. Growing pains as a parent are a real thing, and they may be happening simultaneously with the growth of your children as well. At the start, parenting might feel like a job with clear indicators of success. You may believe that any major issues with your children can be easily prevented, redirected, or solved, trusting that you'll know the signs to watch for and how to address them. But this depends on the assumption that these obvious signs are easy to spot, and that's where the complexity is.

Our mom is someone you want in your corner. If you want someone to be brutally honest with you, to call you out on where you may need to self-reflect and grow, all the while finding the humor in it all, then our mom is the right gal for you. She has two unique talents that few have: the ability to truly see the very best in people, even if they don't see it themselves, and the ability to ignite the flame that pushes people toward their highest selves and, hence, their best relationships.

Our mom has always been our fiercest ally, embodying the spirit of a mother bear. Her talent for offering solutions is matched only by her profound ability to listen. Yet, she has also taught us that the impact of any solution relies not solely on the wisdom of its creator but on the dedication of those who inherit it: us. Knowing better does not always mean doing better. Sometimes, it can feel counterintuitive to let go of certain parenting habits when we're struggling to stay afloat. But if the shore is just within reach, letting go becomes the right thing to do. Our mom is here to help you see it, but only you, however, can decide to swim toward the land. There, you might find your children waiting for you, and at long last, you can begin to sing a new tune of harmony together.

We're thrilled for you to read this book, knowing that having it in your hands means you've taken the first step from wishing to doing! With our mom now in *your* corner, cheering you on, we're confident you're in the best hands. We hope you'll embrace the tools within these pages—ones we sometimes joked we wished she had used with us sooner—and bring them into your own family.

May this book inspire some of your best moments,

Tanner and Autumn

Introduction

So happy you're here!
I hope that this book becomes your trusted companion as you begin this meaningful and fun journey.

> **My Mission:** To empower parents to bring joy to their families, strengthen their relationships, become their children's greatest influence, and inspire them to build a life they love.
> **How:** By equipping parents with a treasure trove of tools. This book is the ultimate toolkit!
> **Why:** Being an inspiring parent is the hardest and most important job on the planet. Every parent deserves support.
> **When:** Now. Every day. I'm here for you.

*Note: In this book, the word "parents" includes all adults who support and contribute to the well-being of a family.

This book is for parents ready to take action and strengthen their family's foundation. All that's needed are the right tools (I've got you covered!) and your willingness to bring desire and discipline to the table (that's on you, but I'm here to help!).

Building strong relationships with your kids starts with a solid foundation—one built on shared values, communication, love, respect, and mutual support. Without such a foundation, building relationships is like trying to construct your dream home on sand—no matter how beautiful it looks from the outside, instability will always creep in. A weak foundation leads to endless repairs and constant uncertainty. Let's work together to build a home—and family—with a strong foundation.

The great news is that you are the architect, foreman, and builder of your family's home. Its strength lies in your capable hands. On this transformative journey, I'll guide you through a treasure trove of timeless tools to help you build a strong family foundation and enjoyable relationships with your kids. And that journey starts with you.

But before we take the plunge together, there are a few things I'd like to share about myself straightaway. This way, you'll get a better sense of who I am and how I roll—my humor, quirks, and why I say things the way I do. The goal is for you to feel my words, not just read them.

So, a bit about me: I'm scrappy, feisty, and fierce. If a crisis hits, you definitely want me on your team. If you need a ride-or-die, or if you're being a bit of an idiot and need a kick in the shins to snap you back to reality—like, pronto—I'm your gal. I'm also generous, thoughtful, and compassionate. You'll want me by your side when it's time to celebrate you, love on you, or feel for you. I'll give you my heart, my time, and anything else you need—within reason. I do love to say "nope."

I'm full of energy, ideas, and relentless tenacity. If you need a brainstorming partner for your wildest dreams or someone to help blowtorch your fears into oblivion, I've got your back. I'll part the Red Sea if that's what it takes to help you achieve your goals.

I'm also an unapologetic animal lover (seriously, I'll save a bee and a squirrel in the same breath) and deeply committed to caring for Mother Earth. You want me around if there's an animal in need or trees to plant. See a dog locked in a hot car? I will absolutely break that window.

I'm a mom, a go-getter, a truth-teller, an Ironman, a lip-sync aficionado, and a bit of a goofball. If you need the hard truth, a clear

Introduction

path forward, or someone to hold you accountable, I'm your coach. I'll help you stay motivated and accountable—all while chortling as much as possible. Laughing is a must.

And just so you know, I'm left-handed. I love that about myself. No real reason for mentioning it; it just felt right to share. I'm certain my fellow southpaws can relate.

With all that said, I hope you can hear me and feel me through these pages as we begin. Consider Parents, Grow Up! as a big hug and a deliberate shove to get you on this journey. Let's get into it.

Getting in the Mood, the Right Mindset

"Parenting without a sense of humor is like being an accountant who sucks at math."
~Amber Dusick

Never truer words spoken. Humor, laughter, and lightheartedness are the treasured trio that's essential to enjoyable and lasting relationships. Because let's be real—parenting? Hardest. Job. Ever. It tests your patience, character, and sanity in ways no one can prepare you for (because seriously, who would sign up if they knew all the gritty details upfront?).

If you've ever felt ineffective as a parent or been tempted to flee for the hills, let me officially welcome you to the Parenting-Can-Suck Club (a.k.a. the What-Have-I-Done? Club). You're not alone; this feeling is universal. Once you become a parent, you automatically qualify for a lifetime membership in the club. Not quite as "awesome" as it sounds...but it can be. I've been a humbled member for almost thirty years.

When my doctor handed me my firstborn after hours of labor, she congratulated me, then said to my husband and me, "Wear a helmet, sit low, fasten your seatbelt, and hold on." We all laughed at the time, not realizing that behind the humor was massive truth.

Here's the comforting part: We're all on this bumpy parenting ride together, facing similar struggles. No matter your challenge—whether it's feeling disrespected by your kids, disconnected from them, or invisible to your family. Or perhaps you feel your only role is the unappreciated provider. Or you're constantly running interference to diffuse family conflict. Or maybe you're just plain exhausted from chronic worry about your children's well-being and future, asking yourself, "Am I doing enough? Am I doing this right?" Or maybe it's the lack of joy and harmony in your home. Or…or…or…the list goes on and on.

I've been there and have experienced all of the above. Every phase of parenting has brought its own set of struggles that require different skill sets and toolkits. This is why I became obsessed with finding ways to strengthen family relationships. I knew every parent was also going through what I was. How I wish I had known then, back when I first became a parent, what I'm about to share with you now.

I've gained vast knowledge by continually learning on the (ever-evolving) job, being in the trenches, and recognizing the profound impact and responsibility my words and actions have had on my kids. I've faced major stumbles, huge setbacks, heaps of failures, and, yes, many regrets. But I chose (and continue to choose) to learn from my mistakes and to do better. I've also experienced the thrill of triumphs and those heart-exploding-with-joy moments when you love them so much you must pinch or hug them—hard.

In addition to being a parent, after a decade working at Apple in the education departments, I forged my own path, creating several empowerment businesses over the last thirty years, including:

- **Chin Up!** Fitness training and coaching for Silicon Valley giants on Sand Hill Road.
- **Ladybug Productions.** An award-winning "All by Myself" empowerment series for toddlers.
- **Life Launch.** A life skills and self-empowerment curriculum for teens and young adults.
- **Online Parent Coaching Course.** A resource for parents seeking guidance and support.

Introduction

- **Family in Flow.** Programs focused on creating harmony within the family ecosystem.

Driven by my tenacity and commitment to strengthening family relationships, I am honored to be a lecturer at the renowned Canyon Ranch Wellness Resorts in Arizona and California. I have a B.A. from San Diego State University and an M.A. in speech communication from the University of Denver.

After years of personal trial and error coupled with my educational background, professional pursuits, and drive to enhance family life, I became an empowerment junkie for teens, young adults, and especially for parents.

And here's what I discovered to be true: It is possible to have a well-connected, respectful, and truly enjoyable relationship with your kids. In fact, it's guaranteed. All you have to do is *stop wishing and start doing*.

Imagine a life where your family relationships are genuinely enjoyable, where daily life brings more ease, and your heart feels full. That's exactly what this book is designed for. It will guide you to become a more fulfilled and peaceful individual while empowering you to be a wiser, more influential, and inspiring leader for your children.

What kind of joy would you feel if your family bonds were stronger? How would it feel to have harmony in the home? To have meaningful, joyful relationships with your kids? Because you're here, I know the quality of your life and the strength of your family's relationships are of tremendous value to you, a priceless and lifelong investment.

I hope that you fully embrace this journey for an empowered you, one that transforms your family through your individual growth. Because if you want real change in your family, you have to start with you—your leadership, your influence, and your commitment to evolve.

The health of any family starts with the health of its leaders: the parental figures. As the leader of your family, it's essential first to strengthen the foundation of who *you* are. This process requires you to get up close and personal with yourself, reflect deeply on the many layers that shape you, and then use the tools found in this book to enhance and improve yourself. Together, we'll explore the culture you've intentionally or unintentionally created within your family. We'll take an honest look at what you've been contributing or contaminating to your family's ecosystem. We'll ask: Are you strengthening or fracturing the foundation of your family's relationships?

I will also introduce you to my Magnificent 8 (M8)—key foundational components designed to help you build a strong, loving family that respects and enjoys one another and empowers you to become the person you're proud to be.

The biggest trap we fall into as parents is believing that, as adults, we've already arrived, that we're done growing and know enough. But the moment we think we've got it all figured out is the moment we close ourselves off from learning, growing, and, most importantly, from connecting with our kids.

To truly grow up as parents, we need to turn up our self-awareness, emotional intelligence, and mental fortitude—not just for family harmony but for our own inner peace. We are, after all, our children's first leaders, teachers, and role models. If we want them to grow into self-confident, independent adults who can build meaningful lives, we must lead the way every single day.

Here's Your New Blueprint

> *"Our kids are inspired by our actions, not our feelings."*
> ~Jill Avery

- **Embrace personal development.** Just because your kids are teens, young adults, or even parents themselves, doesn't mean your growth journey is complete. In fact, your continued personal growth is more important than ever. Parenting at this stage invites you to keep evolving alongside

your children as they grow older. You're never done becoming the best version of yourself, and your continued growth is just as significant as theirs. Let your personal growth lead by example and inspire your kids.
- **Release the need to control everything.** It's natural to want to shield your kids from the inevitable hardships of life or steer them toward what you believe is best. But here's the truth: trying to control their every move or constantly stepping in to fix things only fosters learned helplessness and incompetence. Growth happens when we allow them to face their challenges, take risks, and, yes, fail. You want your kids to gain plenty of experience navigating adversity while they're still under your roof so that they become self-reliant, resourceful, resilient, and adaptable. Trust in their ability to figure things out, even if the path they choose looks different from the one you envisioned. Just like you're still finding your way, they need the freedom to find theirs. Don't deprive them of experiences that build competence and confidence. Let go!
- **Be adaptable.** Parenting teens and young adults is full of unpredictable twists. What worked when they were younger may no longer apply. Stay curious, stay flexible. Be willing to adjust, adapt, and evolve, just as you want your kids to be. You are leading by example.
- **Celebrate who your kids are becoming.** By now, your children are well on their way to becoming individuals with unique talents, dreams, and perspectives. Resist the urge to mold them into who you think they should be or convince them to do what you believe is best. Instead, celebrate who they are. Nurture their passions and strive to be a source of encouragement rather than limitation. Be in awe of their journey, even when it leads them in unexpected directions. Trust that they're creating a life that's authentically theirs and one that will continue to evolve.
- **Cultivate emotional resilience.** Life never stops throwing curveballs. By strengthening your own emotional resilience,

you demonstrate how to handle life's inevitable challenges with grit, grace, and gratitude. Your leading by example becomes a powerful lesson in navigating life's ups and downs for your children, one they'll carry with them long after they've left the nest.

The meaningful feedback and life-changing results from the families I partner with inspired me to write this book so I can reach and empower more families by sharing what I do. You're holding in your hands timeless tools for personal and family transformation. These power tools and practices will not only guide you as you grow and evolve, but they will also teach you how to build a strong and happy family for a lifetime. Keep in mind that personal development, both for yourself and your family, never reaches a finish line.

We'll begin discussing the tools by getting real, by deliberately exposing the many layers of you as prep work to examine and assess the core components of your family's culture. Once you have clarity on what needs improvement, we'll dive into how to take action, guided by the M8. These principles will support you as you grow and reshape how your family functions and interacts.

Once you're rooted in the M8, we'll move on to understanding how your children's brains are wired. This insight will help you avoid setting unrealistic expectations and give you a better understanding of their developmental stages. We'll examine the influence of technology and ways to empower your kids to build healthy relationships with tech in today's digitally dominated world.

We'll also cover the crucial role of trust in families. Trust is earned, and it flows both ways. Your belief in your children is the richest soil for trust to take root and flourish. Cultivating a family culture based on trust is one of the most precious gifts you can give as a family leader. You are responsible for creating and nurturing an

Introduction

environment that feels safe and supportive, which will allow trust to grow.

As you deepen trust, you'll learn how to live a more inspired life, and in doing so, you'll naturally become a source of inspiration for your children. You'll become their greatest influence, leading by example; that's what real inspiration looks like.

Next, I'll equip you with your grab bag, a metaphorical bag filled with resources—reminders, messages, and lessons—that you can grab from to support you in any given situation. Whether you need to ground yourself, make empowered choices, or need more clarity to glean a more productive path or recover from an emotional setback, you'll be prepared for whatever life throws your way.

Finally, we'll pull everything together with a quick review, confirming your readiness to apply these tools, techniques, and mindsets. It's time to turn your newfound knowledge into inspired action. Once you start, huge rewards will head your way.

Here's the thing: none of us stop growing, and that doesn't change when we become parents. In fact, parenting offers some of the biggest opportunities for growth spurts. We're all students in the classroom of life. There are no final exams, but there will be plenty of pop quizzes along the way. And as we grow, so do our families. So, parents, it's time to grow up, again. But this time, do it not just for your kids but for yourself. Your growth? That's fundamental to their future.

Are you ready to get started? Let's begin by getting naked.

Chapter 1
Getting Real, Real Quick

"Don't kid yourself. Be honest with yourself. Take your own inventory."
~Jack Canfield[1]

I hope you're ready because it's time to strip down and get naked!
This is where you must start. It's time to get real with what's holding you back from the person you want to be, the family harmony you crave, and the life you desire. It's showtime! With you, right here, right now. No more hiding, ignoring, procrastinating, blaming, or putting lipstick on the pig.

It's 100 percent up to you whether transformation and positive change happen, and it begins with you getting real and getting raw.

That means you dive deep, silence the noise and distractions, welcome your vulnerability, and be willing to let go of the old belief systems, the gunk you've collected, and the stink that has stuck to you like a fish market.

Sure, you can talk about it all—i.e., your parenting challenges, struggles, failures, etc. with friends and therapists, listen to inspiring podcasts, or even go on those transformational and soul-expanding

---

[1] Jack Canfield, The Success Principles™: How to Get from Where You Are to Where You Want to Be. New York: Collins, 2006.

retreats. But we all know the truth: for change of any kind to happen within your family, it must first start with you. Change happens from the inside out. No more seeking outside of yourself for the answers. The answers are inside you. That's what getting real is all about, and it is the single most significant thing you can do.

Before we dig deeper into the process of getting real with ourselves, let's pause to consider the power our decisions hold. After all, the point of getting real—of seeing who we really are and how we honestly think and feel—is to recognize what needs challenging or changing so we can ultimately make better decisions. Who we are as individuals, the relationships we build with our families, and the life we experience, all flow from the decisions we make. Every decision sets a direction, creates momentum, and brings about a series of consequences and outcomes, for better or worse.

Let me introduce you to the three most impactful decisions we make every moment of every day:

1. What we think,
2. What we feel, and
3. What we do.

The power of these three decisions is often underestimated, overlooked, or even regretted. Yet, these decisions shape the very foundation of our lives. They determine our path and influence everything that follows. As you read this book, I strongly encourage you to bring these decisions into focus. Really reflect on them. Understand their weight and be open to forging a new relationship with them. New BFFs, possibly? Good call!

By doing so, you'll cultivate a habit of honoring these decisions and of recognizing how they shape absolutely *everything* in your life. And here's the most empowering truth of all: your habits are determined by your decisions, and those decisions are entirely up to you.

This realization changed my life and the lives of the people I have (and have had) the privilege to teach. Game-changer? More like *life changer*! That was one of the reasons I was determined to write this book. My deepest desire is to empower you to use these tools to create a strong, connected family, to become a version of yourself you're proud of, and to design a meaningful life, one you are grateful for.

We all have those moments when family life feels off, disconnected, or frustrating. It's part of the deal. But then there are times when everything just clicks, and nothing compares to that joy of being close to your tribe. There's nothing sweeter than when your family is in flow, when all feels right with the world. If you skip getting real with yourself, you'll never feel truly comfortable in your own skin. You'll feel like an imposter, a fake, a fraud. You'll block your own personal growth and squander your innate gifts and talents. Frankly, the cost of *not* getting real might just be the foundation of your family. Oh, the power you hold!

Here's the magic: When you get real, you connect with your true self, and then there's a surrender that happens within your mind and body. With this newfound clarity, you can finally let go of the mental and emotional baggage you've been hauling around. You'll experience a much-needed exhale and feel your shoulders drop as if they're finally saying, "Ah, about time."

The lightness of this letting go opens the door to your inner liberation and self-empowerment. The release of this emotional and mental weight now provides the needed space for your new mindset to take root, grow, and flourish. As we know, if we don't acknowledge, address, and put to rest the trauma, guilt, shame, stress, anxiety, and anger we carry, they will wreak havoc on us not only physically but also mentally, emotionally, and spiritually. They will seep into every part of our lives. One of my taglines is: "When you're well, the whole world benefits, especially your family." No one gets a free pass from hardship and tragedy, but we do have choices. We have plenty of productive and helpful paths to choose from if we decide to take them. And it all circles back to our decisions. We hold the power to choose.

Parents, Grow Up!

> *"The beginning is the most important part of the work."*
> ~Plato[2]

Ready? Let's Lean in...

So, to start getting real, let's zoom out and talk about the gunk and the goods you've collected throughout your life, intentionally or not. This includes examining how you were raised, your belief systems, attitudes, and what you value. All of these have absolutely shaped who you are, how you behave, and why you do what you do. Whether you resisted or embraced your parents' belief systems, attitudes, or values, they've impacted you. We all have these layers (and we'll dive deeper into this later), and we bring them into our own parenting style and our family's ecosystem, consciously or not.

When you clear away the gunk and get real about the many layers that make up who you are, you gain tremendous courage and clarity. Courage gives you the strength to be honest with yourself, which is not easy, and to take accountability. Clarity reveals what you're contributing or contaminating within your family's ecosystem. When you're aware of what you bring to the table and how that influences your family's ecosystem, you can begin to create meaningful change, starting with yourself. By shifting how you think, feel, communicate, and act, you can spark a remarkable transformation within your family. It always begins with you. As the leader, your family looks to you for guidance and strength.

For example, if you let your explosive emotions do all the talking with your family, getting real with yourself will help you uncover why you react that way and where those behaviors are coming from. Getting real means having the guts to stand in truth. Not the kind of truth that justifies, excuses, or defends your unhealthy behaviors, but the raw, courageous truth. It's not easy, but it's incredibly

---

2 Plato. *The Republic: The Complete and Unabridged Jowett Translation* (Vintage Classics)

empowering and freeing. Once you're aware, you can make the necessary changes to improve yourself, which, of course, benefits your entire family. There will be no more emotional outbursts. You now take a pause, take a breath, reset yourself, and lead by example with productive communication. Your family will feel this energetic shift within the ecosystem of your home. Instead of creating friction or fear, you'll provide true leadership and a nurturing environment. Your children's anxiety and stress will diminish, or even disappear, not because they've changed, but because you have. By contributing nourishment to your family's ecosystem, you fortify its foundation and relationships, empowering your children through your leadership. This is what it means to lead by example. To get real, you'll begin by exploring the many layers of who you are.

The Many Layers of You

Let's get real about your many layers.

These layers make us who we are and determine how we show up for ourselves, our families, and the world. Within each layer, we have naturally accumulated baggage throughout our life experiences. This isn't wrong or bad—it's called being human. Now, with that said, don't let "being human" become an excuse to cling to your baggage. Instead, see it as an opportunity to grow—we're all students of life.

So the question isn't, do you have baggage? The questions are: Are you aware of the baggage you're carrying? Do you understand how it's affecting your children, your relationships, and the quality of your life? Because here's the deal: what you're not aware of, you can't change.

It's impossible to get real when you're detached from your self-awareness. Detachment is a coping mechanism, a way to block ourselves from the things we find painful, difficult, or dangerous. But here's the catch: When you detach from yourself, you're not just detaching from the painful feelings; you're also cutting yourself off from the positive feelings. Detachment can numb your ability to feel, period. That's why it's so important to understand your relationship with detachment; it can create unintended consequences that ripple through your life. By exploring the many layers of who you are, you can begin to reconnect with yourself, so you can then reshape and rebuild into a stronger, healthier you.

The layers we'll explore are your ego, habits, society, family history and patterns, belief systems, and core values. Keep in mind: the deeper you "get real," the greater the liberation you'll feel. Approach this process with the patience and honesty you deserve.

Ego

Egos often get a bad rap, usually because of the over-inflated, "all about me" stereotype. But everyone has an ego—your sense of self, the inner voice that shapes how you see yourself and how you believe others see you. It influences your thoughts, behaviors, and relationships, including how you show up as a parent. Begin by asking the tough questions you'd rather avoid: What is your relationship with your ego? How does it show up within your family?

For example, do you have quiet confidence in your ability to lead your family? Or do you need to control every detail? Do you get offended easily when your family disagrees with you, or do you welcome different opinions as a chance to understand their perspectives better? It's time to get up close and personal with your ego and make it your friend, not your foe.

Habits

The good, the bad, and the downright ugly. Habits are the repeated actions that shape our lives, bringing us closer to or pulling us further from our ideal selves. Habits are the behaviors, rituals, and routines we do so regularly that they become automatic.

Whether they're thoughts, responses, reactions, or actions, habits hold incredible power. Don't underestimate them. But don't forget, you gave life to your habits through commitment and consistency, so you also hold the power to change them. Take a closer look at the habits behind your thoughts, feelings, and actions. When we think of habits, we often focus on the easier and obvious ones like eating, drinking, sleeping, or exercising—things we do to ourselves. Those absolutely play a big role in your parental leadership and can impact your family. But it's also important to dig deeper and examine the habitual thoughts and beliefs that shape your parenting and influence your relationship with your kids. Do you always need to be right? Feel the need for the last word? Do your words align with your actions? Do you withdraw from conflict or insist on doing things your way to feel respected? Or do you placate and appease to avoid friction? These patterns deserve your attention. They can impact not just you but your entire family dynamic.

Get real with the habits you've created and decide their fate. Choose them wisely and dump them wisely. Habits create your future and define the quality of your life.

Society

In the age of digital dominance, societal pressures have taken on new forms, significantly shaping how we raise our kids and evolve as families. It appears we are not only trying to keep up but also trying to measure up. That is, instead of keeping up with the Joneses, we want to outdo and dominate the Joneses. The Fear of Missing Out (FOMO) took on a whole new meaning when social media blanketed the world. We are now living in a world I call F.A.S.T.—a world of fear, anxiety, stress, and technology.

Consider the compare-and-despair mental state, doom-scrolling depression, and thirst traps, and ask: What is your relationship with societal pressures and expectations? Are you caught in the madness of the masses, or have you put healthy boundaries in place to keep yourself grounded? Take an honest look at your relationship with social media. Evaluate what you consume, how it affects you, and what you're putting out there for the world to interpret, perceive, or judge. How do you feel after seeing what everyone else is doing, buying, wearing, or where they're going? Maybe it's time for a cleanse?

Family History and Patterns

Family history and patterns run deep and wide. History loves to repeat itself, doesn't it? The traditions, beliefs, attitudes, and values our parents passed down to us are often deeply rooted, whether we're aware of it. And like it or not, we bring pieces of our own childhood into our parenting. Some of those pieces? Pure gold. Others? Well, let's just say, what didn't kill us definitely made us stronger...yeah, we'll go with that.

So, what influences from your own upbringing have found their way into your family's ecosystem? It's time to get real and do a quality check. Was toxic communication a norm? Were children expected to be seen and not heard? Were your parents perfectionistic, overly strict, or too lenient? Was money a constant worry that became your worry, too? Did you experience physical, mental, or emotional abuse? Or did growing up with privilege shape expectations for having the finer things?

You can break unhealthy family patterns and create a positive new legacy. Getting real is where the breakthroughs start and where real change begins.

Belief Systems

Our beliefs are the assumptions and opinions we hold as truth, shaped by past experiences and the cultural and environmental influences we've encountered. Let's be honest. Beliefs can divide us, especially when it comes to the usual suspects: religion, race, politics, culture, nationality, and socioeconomic status. These beliefs can grip us tightly, sometimes like a chokehold.

As we grow and evolve, it's important to revisit and reassess our beliefs. We become what we believe.

Do you believe formal education is the only path to success and respect? Is following your passion less important than playing it safe with a stable job? Do you live by the mantra "happy wife, happy life"? Or believe you're "right" simply because you're the parent?

It's time to get real about how your beliefs are shaping you and your family.

Getting Real, Real Quick

Core Values

Values are those universal threads that come from the experience of being human. Think: integrity, trustworthiness, kindness, honesty, compassion, and gratitude, those kinds of gems. Unlike beliefs, values tend to unite us because of their positive, inclusive nature. What we value shapes who we are and the direction we take in life. Yet, while most people *think* they have core values, their actions often tell a different story. As I like to remind the parents I coach, "If you don't value your values, they have no value."

So, ask: Are your core values really guiding and serving you, or are they just collecting dust?

These "many layers" shape who we are, how we act, and why we do what we do. It's time to get real. Take a good, honest look at each layer through a clear lens and ask yourself, "What am I bringing to the table? And what chaos might I be creating?" In other words, how are you contributing positively, and where might you be contaminating your family's ecosystem? Be brave, lean in, and be honest. Your growth depends on it, and so does your family's!

Please don't skip this part. Ask yourself these tough questions, dig deep, and get real with what makes you, you. Take your time. Don't rush. The deeper you go, the more you'll learn and understand. Remember, you're the leader of your family, and your leadership has a significant impact on them. Can you handle the truth? I believe you can, and you must.

Family Culture: The Heartbeat of Your Home

Let's take a closer look at the culture that shapes your family—the unique values, habits, and dynamics that define how your home feels and functions. As I often tell the parents I work with, "Tell me about your family's culture, and I'll tell you about the strength of your relationships and the foundation beneath them." Surprisingly, many people don't even think of their family as having a culture. But trust me, every family does. It's the invisible fabric woven from how you all think, feel, and act and what you hold dear. And guess what? Your kids are soaking it all up, building their own sense of right and wrong from this rich (or tattered) tapestry.

Take a moment to reflect on your own upbringing. How did the environment you grew up in shape who you are, both back then and now that you're a parent?

Was your home filled with music and the aroma of home-cooked meals? Is that something you do now in your own home? Or were you a latchkey kid? Home alone and responsible for making dinner? Maybe you give your kids the same responsibility because that's how you were raised. Was your house the go-to hangout spot because it felt welcoming and had good snacks? Did you subsequently roll this into your family's culture? Or did you avoid bringing friends over because it was messy, and your parents weren't exactly thrilled? Was your home like a mini-zoo full of dogs, cats, birds, and guinea pigs? Or did you have no pets at all because they were considered too much trouble? And how do you feel about having animals in your home now?

Like most things in life, family culture isn't set in stone. It evolves as you do. That's why it's so important to pause every now and then and ask: Is your home a place where you nurture one another? Are you building healthy relationships? Does your environment support your well-being and what truly matters to your family? Because at the end of the day, there's no place like home, sweet home, the space where your family's story unfolds.

Now that you've reflected on how your past might be influencing your parenting, let's dive into what shapes your family's culture. I'll introduce you to the eight core elements that define it so you can be more intentional about the environment you're creating.

Hey! Heads up! The eight elements below are designed to strengthen your family one step at a time. There is no need to freak out or feel like you're late to the game. Pick one, give it some love, and then move to the next. Think of these as layers in your family's foundation, each one making things stronger, more secure, and rock-solid over time.

Getting Real, Real Quick

1. Family Values

Family values reveal your tribe's priorities, create structure, and provide a moral code. They shape the culture of your family, influencing the way you communicate, solve problems, and support one another. Think: honesty, faith, education, loyalty, family time, accountability, care for the planet, and trustworthiness. These are not just abstract concepts but guiding principles that, when truly embraced, shape your family's identity and the legacy you leave behind.

Your family values determine the choices you make in times of crisis, the way you celebrate successes, and how you overcome challenges together. Values such as honesty might lead to open and transparent communication within the family, while a commitment to education could prioritize learning and growth, both academically and personally. Remember, values that aren't valued are worthless. Talk is cheap; actions speak louder. It's not enough to simply profess your family values; they must be woven into the fabric of your daily life, reflected in both small choices and big decisions. These lived values shape not only your family's present but also the legacy you pass down to future generations.

So, what are your family values? Do you genuinely live by them? Honor them? Or are they just things you say to make yourself feel better or to impress others?

2. Family Traditions

Family traditions are the customs passed down by your parents, grandparents, and ancestors, plus the new ones you create with your kids. These rituals and practices are often loaded with deep cultural, religious, or personal significance, reflecting the values and beliefs that have shaped your family's history over generations. For instance, how do you celebrate birthdays? Do you have special meals, unique ways of giving gifts, or specific activities that are part of the celebration? How do you honor funerals? Perhaps you follow certain rituals, like lighting candles, gathering for a special meal, or visiting gravesites on significant dates. How do you observe holidays? From

Christmas to Diwali, Easter to Passover, the way you celebrate these moments often involves a blend of inherited traditions and newly formed customs that reflect your family's unique personality.

Additionally, what traditions mark milestones like the first day of school, graduations, or weddings? These might include taking pictures in the same spot each year, holding a special dinner, or giving a meaningful gift. Or perhaps it's a rousing game of charades every Thanksgiving after dessert. Traditions such as these provide structure and predictability for your family's life. They are the threads that weave your family's story together, linking past, present, and future in a continuous narrative.

These traditions are important in creating cherished memories and fostering a sense of unity and continuity within the family. Those cherished memories are then often passed on to future generations, evolving yet preserving the essence of the family's identity. Whether grand or simple, inherited or newly made, these traditions help to reinforce a strong foundation for family life.

3. Family Rituals

Family rituals are activities families do together, whether every day, once a week, or once a month; they occur more frequently than traditions. They are unique to each family, like a quick after-meal walk around the neighborhood, dedicating Wednesdays to being pizza-and-pajama nights or creating Sandwich Sundays because food somehow always seems to bring people together, or sharing a special phrase, handshake, or hug before heading out the door each morning. Or maybe it's a bedtime ritual after brushing teeth—such as reading a book, sharing a short story, or expressing a few things to be thankful for. Family rituals help strengthen bonds and reinforce the culture you want for your family. They act as anchors, offering a sense of continuity and belonging.

Rituals create connections and camaraderie, allowing each family member to feel valued and integral to the whole. They're patterned activities that bring comfort, consistency, and predictability, providing a safe haven amongst the unpredictability of life. Whether it's having dinner together every night, sharing Saturday morning walks with the dog(s), or enjoying Sunday bagels before starting household chores, these moments serve as touchstones that can be passed down through generations.

In addition, rituals offer an opportunity to support the family's values, teach life lessons, and cultivate lasting memories. They are smaller, intimate moments that reinforce family bonds in daily life. Indeed, rituals are righteous!

4. Family Beliefs

Family beliefs act as the guiding compass of life, forming the bedrock of how we perceive the world. They shape everything from daily decisions—such as our views on nutrition, including veganism, kosher, or dairy-free diets—to major life choices, like opting for a secure career versus pursuing a passion.

Beliefs define our values and behavior, guiding us through the messy, wonderful chaos that is family life. But beliefs can be dicey. They're based on opinions, and, like the time you made up your mind and swore you'd never wear that old sweater again, they change. Sometimes drastically. That's because, as we gain knowledge and experience, our beliefs evolve—for instance, trading in the belief that "success demands keeping our nose to the grindstone" for something more balanced (and let's face it, more realistic) such as "be where your feet are: be present, enjoy the moment."

Think of beliefs as lenses through which we view the world. Some might help us see the bigger picture, while others? Let's just say they need a prescription change. Remember the saying, "Make love, not war"? That embodies a belief in diffusing conflict with love and peace, which is much easier to embrace when you're well-rested and not stuck in traffic, about to miss your flight. Or how about "optimism over realism"? That's for those of us who prefer to see the glass half full, even if it's clearly leaking from the bottom. And let's not forget how beliefs define our political identities. Conservative, liberal, independent: those labels are tied to a belief system.

Family beliefs tackle the big stuff like religion, equal rights, animal rights, and environmental advocacy. These aren't just topics for debate around the dinner table; they influence the choices we make as a team and the way we see and navigate the world.

Here's the thing: we need to be willing to examine our beliefs honestly and without defensiveness. Personal growth often requires admitting we've been holding onto outdated ideas—kind of like that treadmill we swore we'd use every day but now just sits in the corner doubling as a coat rack. It takes real introspection to figure out if our beliefs align with who we are today. Were these ideas adopted because they truly resonated with us, or are they leftovers from childhood or societal influence? It's easy to become emotionally attached to our beliefs (like fiercely defending why I believe jalapeño peppers make bolognese sauce so much better), but if we cling too tightly, we restrict our ability to appreciate diverse perspectives and experiences that can expand our understanding of the world.

Family beliefs are more than just personal; they shape the identity of the entire family. They're powerful tools that can either broaden our horizons or narrow our vision. The key is to be intentional about what we believe, cultivating our beliefs with care and wisdom.

5. Family Attitudes

Your family's attitude is a mirror reflecting its collective mindset, shaping how each member interacts with the world and with each other. Family attitudes originate from the parents. Kids are born into these attitudes, which significantly influence their behaviors, values, and relationships.

Attitudes encompass ways of thinking, feeling, and acting. To greatly improve your family's culture, attitude is a crucial area to focus on. Are you optimistic or skeptical? Straight shooters or storytellers? Cautious or risk-takers? Is your family love-based, nurturing connections with warmth and support, or fear-based, driven by stress, doom and gloom, and skepticism? Are you a family of hotheads who react impulsively, or are you people pleasers who avoid conflict at all costs? Do you approach life with a thirst for knowledge, open to learning and growing, or do you operate as a know-it-all, closed off to new ideas? Speaking of which, how's your attitude right now? Are you open to learning something new, or do you feel you already know what I'm sharing?

Attitudes shape not just your outlook but the essence of your family's identity.

6. Home Environment

When I refer to the home environment, I mean the overall conditions and factors present in a household. It's how your home looks, feels, and functions. This includes the cleanliness of the home, the emotional atmosphere, and how the house and space are cared for and arranged to promote safety, security, a relaxed heart, and a curious mind.

What does your home environment feel like? Is it calm and cozy, a sanctuary where you can unwind and recharge? Or is it stressful and chaotic, where tension lingers in the air? Perhaps it feels sterile and cold, lacking warmth and personality, or maybe it's creative and musical, filled with the vibrancy of artistic expression. Or does your home seem to be in a state of chronic repair, causing worry and strain?

Ideally, home should embody safety, security, and stability, a place where you feel truly at ease. But beyond just casually observing, consider the subtle details: the lighting, the sounds, the scents, and the overall ambiance. How do these elements contribute to the atmosphere of your home? Are there areas that could use a touch of warmth, color, or organization?

Strive to make "home sweet home" not just a saying but a lived reality and a sense of belonging. Remember, your home environment is not just about physical surroundings but also about the emotional and psychological space it creates for you and your loved ones. That means your home cultivates a supportive atmosphere where everyone feels comfortable expressing themselves, setting aside time for family conversations or activities that strengthen relationships, and ensuring that each person has their personal space to retreat and recharge. By focusing on these elements, you create a home where emotional well-being and mental peace thrive alongside physical comfort.

7. Family Priorities

Family priorities are the areas that a family deems most important and decides to focus on. Priorities reflect and support your values and beliefs.

So, what are your family's priorities? What do you deem important as a family? Staying active and eating healthy? Spending quality time together? Being community-minded and volunteering? Traveling to explore other cultures?

When priorities are set, they serve as a guiding star, helping your family navigate decisions big and small, ensuring that your collective actions are in harmony with your shared values. For instance, if a priority is health and wellness, then family activities might include preparing nutritious meals together, engaging in physical activities like hiking or cycling, and fostering a home environment where healthy living is encouraged and celebrated. If education is a priority, creating a culture of learning by reading together, supporting each other's academic goals, and exploring new skills as a family might be at the forefront.

Involving all family members in the process of setting these priorities is crucial. It not only ensures that everyone feels heard and valued but also boosts collective morale. When everyone has a stake in determining the family's direction, there's a greater sense of commitment and responsibility toward maintaining those priorities. If you haven't set your family's priorities yet, take the time to get together and decide. Doing this fosters a deeper connection and helps create a roadmap for a fulfilling and meaningful life together. Having clearly defined family priorities creates a sense of camaraderie and purpose that aligns every member with common goals.

8. Family Goals

As the saying goes, "Goals without a plan are just wishes." I like to add, "A plan that's not acted upon becomes a regret." Family goals are shared desires and endeavors that family members agree upon and choose to work toward together. They lay out a plan for what your family wants to achieve together, fostering a sense of unity and direction.

Whether they're weekly, monthly, quarterly, or yearly goals, set them and stick to them. These goals can be as simple as trying a new restaurant on the last Saturday of each month or as ambitious as planning a family vacation to hike in the Grand Canyon. The key is not just to set the goals but to follow through on them.

When goals are set, they should be specific, measurable, achievable, relevant, and time-bound (SMART). That ensures that the goals are clear and that progress can be tracked, giving the family a sense of accomplishment as they achieve each milestone. For example, suppose your family sets a goal to ban cell phones during meals for the month of March. It might be helpful to discuss why this goal is important—perhaps it's to improve communication and presence at the dinner table, which would make it relevant. Then, you could set up reminders or create a fun challenge to keep everyone on track. Family goals can also focus on personal growth and development, such as learning a new skill together, volunteering as a family, or even adopting a new hobby like gardening or cooking. These activities help achieve the goal, strengthen family bonds, and create lasting memories.

It's also important to regularly review and adjust the goals as needed. Life is dynamic, and family circumstances change, so being flexible and open to revising goals ensures they remain relevant and attainable. Additionally, celebrating the achievement of goals, no matter how small, is crucial for maintaining motivation and reinforcing the value of working together as a family. Keep in mind that the process of setting and working toward goals is just as important as the end result because it teaches valuable life skills such as planning, persistence, and teamwork while also providing the family with a shared sense of achievement. So, whatever the goal, make it meaningful, follow through, and enjoy the journey together.

With a deeper understanding of family culture, you can create one that nourishes, empowers, and fortifies. Your family culture is always at play, shaping your children's childhood and adulthood. These cultural layers are imprinted on your kids, leaving a lasting mark on their hearts and minds. Improving relationships and fostering harmony starts with what you bring to the table.

But before you can get real with your family's culture, you first must get real with yourself. Only then can you create a nourished and connected tribe. Your family's culture starts with your leadership.

Let's keep on rolling...

Indulge me and picture this: I stand perched at the peak of the tallest mountain, one foot on the very edge, hands on my hips, chin up, gazing across the vast horizon. My superhero cape—because of course, I'm wearing one—rippling in slow motion from the wind like I was born for this moment. Then, with the voice of James Earl Jones (a few octaves higher), I command, "The Magnificent 8!"

Chapter 2
The Magnificent 8

"The joy is not in the victory or in standing at the top of the mountain. The joy is the work that gets you there."
~Arnold Schwarzenegger[3]

Fellow travelers, this is the moment we've all been waiting for—or really, the moment I have been waiting for! Behold The Magnificent 8 (M8)!

Born out of my countless hours of empowerment coaching, guiding everyone from high school students to professionals at the top of their game, the M8 has emerged as a bulletproof, universal toolkit for transforming lives. Over the years, I realized I was consistently leaning on the same eight powerful principles, mindsets, practices, and frameworks that formed a rock-solid foundation. This foundation didn't just help; it's been the catalyst for epic transformations. And now, I'm here to share it with you, to spark that same shift in your life.

For those who've joined forces with the M8, the results have been nothing short of legendary. Yes, this is quite the build-up, and the M8

---

[3] Arnold Schwarzenegger, *77 Lessons at 77*, 2024.

has earned every bit of it. Witnessing the lives of teens, young adults, and parents transform through their steadfast commitment to the M8 can only be described in heroic terms: epic and legendary.

Now, before you think this is some magic trick, let's get real. The M8 *only* works because of these three simple reasons (simple rarely means easy):

1. **You must believe in the M8.** When you believe in something, you're all in. It becomes a guiding force in your actions and decisions.
2. **You consistently take action with the M8.** Mastery isn't a fluke; it's the result of steady practice until those skills feel as natural as breathing.
3. **You make the M8 a lifestyle.** This isn't a quick fix. It's a lifelong commitment, a deliberate choice to show up every day with intention.

The M8 isn't about flash or excitement. It's about results. Like a seatbelt, its purpose is crystal clear, not thrilling, but it can save lives. Yours and the lives of those you love.

As we know, when we have a goal attached to a system or plan, we can generate traction by the action we take. That is, when we commit, we put energy and effort forth, which creates momentum; this momentum is where ideas, thoughts, and decisions turn into action. To truly live, you must act. You must lean into your life facing forward. To remain stuck and idle out of fear, procrastination, or laziness will cost you one of the most precious and finite resources of all: *your time*. Tick-tock goes the clock. To feel alive, we must progress and evolve. The M8 gets you to take action and live the life you have dreamed of.

I hope you are feeling giddy about the power and the goodness that awaits you if you dare to value who you are and treasure your time here. It's now time to begin redesigning and strengthening your inner infrastructure: your brain (mindset), which is the command center; your heart, which is your emotional center; and your soul,

The Magnificent 8

which is your truth center. This is where the M8 becomes your inner network, supporting who, what, why, and how you are.

The M8 is a set of intangible tools you can carry around forever. They are light as air, they don't require any physical space, you'll never lose them, and they will always serve and empower you when you use them.

Each component of the M8 has the potential to spark extraordinary change all on its own. They're like standalone superheroes of wisdom. You don't have to master all eight at once to start experiencing remarkable transformation within yourself. Take your time with each one. Get to know their strengths, understand their unique powers, and gradually integrate them into your daily life, one by one.

I suggest you focus on one at a time, letting it weave into the fabric of your everyday routine. As you delve deeper into each of the M8 components, you'll discover how they naturally align, support, and amplify one another. Their brilliance lies in their seamless interconnectedness, creating a powerful synergy that elevates every part of your life. When that happens, you'll feel a tangible shift in your energy and ecosystem. Trust me, that's the kind of power and impact the M8 holds. You'll feel calm, competent, confident, and grounded. And really, who doesn't want that? So, let's get to it.

The Magnificent 8

1. Put Your Oxygen Mask on First

If you don't take care of yourself, you can't take care of your family, just as the flight attendant instructs, "Put your oxygen mask on first." That metaphor is a powerful reminder in everyday life to take care of yourself first, breathe, and catch your breath before responding, deciding, or acting. Breathing is the essence of life, always there to be your Zen Master or Energizer. When you feel stressed or out of balance, taking a deep breath will bring you back to center, calming your mind and body and allowing wiser decisions.

A powerful technique is Dr. Andrew Weil's 4-7-8 method. He has wonderful instructional videos to teach you this technique step by step. In short, this is how you do it. First, inhale through your nose for a count of four, hold for a count of seven, then exhale out your mouth for a count of eight. Repeat four times. (Note: Never perform this while driving or operating any type of machinery.) Many of my clients experience profound physical and mental shifts with this practice. Master it and make it your lifelong ally. Start and end your day with mindful breathing, letting each breath create a calmer and more grounded you. This has become a favorite daily ritual for me.

2. Begin with the End in Mind

Stephen Covey's sage advice, "Begin with the end in mind," is a simple yet powerful way to bring clarity and focus to your day. I use this multiple times a day, and without fail, it keeps my purpose lit and my direction clear. When you ask yourself, "What is the result I want? What's my goal?" and "What's the purpose?" immediately, a pathway is illuminated. This approach helps you decide what to say yes or no to as you work toward your desired outcome.

Whether it's creating special moments with family, reaching a personal goal, or navigating a difficult situation, starting with a clear vision keeps you focused on what really matters. For example, if your goal is a fun, relaxed family picnic, you'll naturally avoid any sensitive or controversial topics during that event. Instead, you will focus on making the day enjoyable. Let the clarity of your desired outcome guide your choices and help ensure the path you take is as rewarding as the goal itself.

3. If It Is to Be, It Is Up to Me

This component is outrageously special to me and deserves extra space and the spotlight. There's a certain power in words, a power that can shape destinies, shift perspectives, and ignite a fire within the soul. Among all the words in the world, ten of the simplest, most unassuming two-letter words hold a transformative magic. I'll never forget the day these words found their way into my life, stuck to my

The Magnificent 8

soul, and forever changed how I saw myself, the world, and my place in it.

I was in third grade, just eight years old, sitting at my desk in the second row behind my best friend, Marnie. It was an ordinary day until our teacher, Mrs. Hitchings, did something extraordinary. With a deliberate, almost theatrical slowness, she began walking among our desks, capturing every single kid's attention. Her eyes met each of ours with a mesmerizing intensity, and in a voice as soft as a secret but as sincere as a promise, she said, "Can I share a secret with all of you? Something so magical and so powerful that it could become one of your superpowers for the rest of your lives?"

As if a spell had been cast, every single one of us was drawn in. We leaned forward, elbows pressed into our desks, our bodies tense with anticipation. I remember gripping the edge of my desk so tightly that my fingers ached. The more she spoke, the more we were enraptured, pulled into her world of magic and mystery. Marnie turned to me, her face a mirror of my own excitement: wide-eyed, grinning, caught somewhere between exhilaration and impatience.

Mrs. Hitchings made her way back to the front of the classroom, the suspense building with each step. "What I'm about to share with you," she said, sitting on the edge of her desk, "are the ten most powerful two-letter words you'll ever know. These words carry lifelong magical powers when you believe in them."

At that moment, you could feel the collective tension. Twenty-eight kids on the edges of their seats, ready to burst with anticipation. Mrs. Hitchings leaned forward as if she were about to reveal the secrets of the universe itself. And then, with a gravity that felt almost sacred, she said, "Are you ready?" The room erupted with a variety of bizarre sounds, noises that only tightly wound third graders could produce. She took that as a yes.

As she leaned toward us, we leaned toward her. And then, very slowly and very clearly, she revealed the secret: "The ten most powerful two-letter words: if it is to be, it is up to me."

She let the words hang in the air, their significance sinking deep into our young minds. She repeated them again and again, each time with incredible care, as if she were handing us a precious gift. Mrs. Hitchings didn't just say the words; she made them come alive. She didn't write the phrase on the chalkboard because, as she said, it was a secret. Instead, she made us repeat them back to her over and over, programming our young, impressionable brains. She then asked us, "Do you know what this means? Do you understand the superpowers these words give you?" None of us could speak. We just nodded furiously, desperate for her to continue, to unlock more of the mystery.

I don't remember her exact words after that, but I knew right then and there that I would never forget that moment for the rest of my life. Mrs. Hitchings spoke to us as if we were the chosen ones, as if we were superheroes in training, and these ten two-letter words were the keys to defeating any kryptonite life might throw our way.

From that day forward, those words were more than just a phrase. They were a mantra, a guiding principle, a source of strength. They became our invisible superhero capes, something we could wrap around ourselves in moments of doubt and fear. They made us believe that we were capable of anything and could conquer any challenge, any obstacle, simply by believing in ourselves. Full ownership of our decisions. Full responsibility for our actions. Full accountability for our lives.

That day in the fall of 1972, my life was transformed by a teacher who believed in me. In room 28, my sense of self-worth was born; my self-confidence was ignited. The ten most powerful two-letter words became my foundation and how I have lived an empowered life since. I share this story because it reveals the profound power of belief, both in ourselves and in others. The power of words and the impact of their delivery. And who knows? Maybe, just maybe, these words will be as magical for you as they still are for me.

4. Desire and Discipline: The Dynamic Duo

Desire and discipline are like the James Bond and Q of success: they're the ultimate team when it comes to getting things done. When these two team up, achieving your goals isn't just possible; it's inevitable. Imagine you're set on becoming a great tennis player. Desire alone won't cut it if you don't have the discipline to practice daily, don't get a coach to keep you improving, and don't push yourself beyond your comfort zone. Conversely, all the discipline in the world won't make you a champion if your heart's not in the game. No surprises there. That's why I call them the dynamic duo; you need both in your corner. Sure, willpower is great, but it's like a match. It burns bright, then fizzles out. Motivation? Also awesome, but it's a fickle friend. So, ignite your desire, fire up that discipline, and get the results you came for.

5. The 4 A's: A Framework for Clarity and Productivity

I didn't just stumble upon the 4 A's; I lived them. They became my go-to method for cutting through the noise and finding a clear, wise path forward. The 4 A's are simple yet powerful: they offer a system for accountability, clarity, and making smarter decisions. Here's how they break down:

1. **Awareness.** It all starts here. You can't fix what you're blind to. Recognize what's not working, and you're already on your way to improvement.
2. **Acknowledge.** Own it. Admitting there's an issue is the first step toward accountability. It's where change begins.
3. **Assess.** Time to dig in. What are you doing that's helping, and what's holding you back? This step reveals what's fueling your progress and what's throwing a wrench in the works. Assess what is contributing positively and what's contaminating.
4. **Action.** Armed with your assessment, you're ready to act. Take action with what works and ditch what doesn't, and you'll make wiser, more productive decisions moving forward.

The beauty of the 4 A's is that you can apply them to just about anything—habits, beliefs, behaviors, you name it. Let's take my own experience as an example. I can be a bit controlling (understatement of the year). Here's how I ran that trait through the 4 A's:

- **Awareness.** I'm fully aware that I have a strong need to be in control and in charge, and I hold the reins too tightly, especially in my family.
- **Acknowledge.** I admit that my controlling behavior causes friction and stress within my family. It's time to take accountability and change my behavior.
- **Assess.** I looked at the positives and negatives of my boss-lady attitude.
  - Positives: I get things done. I am driven to help, provide leadership, and make solid decisions.
  - Negatives: I create stress, my kids feel bulldozed, and I give the impression that I don't trust in their abilities.
- **Action.** Moving forward, I'll be more inclusive and flexible. I'll create opportunities for my kids to step up and be involved, and I'll learn to let go of the reins a bit. It's my job to lead by example and to be open to learning from my family.

The 4 A's process isn't a one-and-done deal. It's more like an artichoke. With each leaf of an artichoke you pluck, you get closer to the heart where the good stuff is. So, don't rush it. Be honest with yourself, even when it's uncomfortable. The act of self-improvement is not supposed to be fun. It's about the rewards you'll receive because of your commitment.

As you practice the 4 A's, you'll start to see and feel a shift in yourself and in the way your energy impacts those around you. You'll feel lighter, clearer, and more empowered.

Remember, the 4 A's can apply to anything—a thought, a feeling, a habit, or a decision. The more you use them, the more they'll become your go-to for a better, more intentional life.

6. Pain of Regret or Pain of Discipline

Jim Rohn nailed it when he said, "We must all suffer from one of two pains: the pain of discipline or the pain of regret. The difference is discipline weighs ounces while regret weighs tons."[4] The choice? It's all yours.

This tool is for taking a pause, thinking, feeling, and choosing a wiser path forward. Think back on the three most important decisions you make every single moment, every single day, that determine the quality and direction of your life: what you think, feel, and do. With each of those comes a choice: do you want the light sting of discipline now or the crushing weight of regret later? When you fold this concept into your mindset, you're setting yourself up to make wiser decisions—not just today but for a lifetime. Every moment allows you to choose.

So, the next time you're at a crossroads, ask yourself: "Which pain do I want to live with?" Remember, one is temporary, and the other can linger for a lifetime.

7. JED Is Dead

Let's talk about JED. No, not Jed from the Beverly Hillbillies. This JED stands for justify, excuse, and defend. When you catch yourself JEDing, whether in your mind or in a conversation with someone else, it's a big, flashing neon sign that you're hitting on something that needs a bit more truth from you. JED has a sneaky way of revealing our insecurities and fears.

When you're feeling confident, grounded, and in alignment with your higher self and the truth, there's no need for JED. But when you find yourself diving into the Justify, Excuse, and Defend routine, it's a signal that it's time for a little introspection.

Here's a quick example: imagine you're late to a meeting. Your first instinct might be to say, "Well, traffic was terrible," or "My alarm didn't go off." But those are justifications and excuses. Instead, try owning it: "My apologies for being late. I'll do better next time." See the difference? No JEDing. This concept is a favorite among my friends and students, and trust me, now that you know about JED,

---

[4] https://www.youtube.com/shorts/hqqT_PViUMI

you'll hear it everywhere, both in others and yourself. Practicing JED is dead will save a lot of your breath and time.

8. Humor

HUMOR is more than just a word; it's an acronym I created: heartful, upbeat, mindful, optimistic, and respectful. These are the pillars of good humor. When humor reflects these values, it avoids the hurtful jabs disguised as jokes or the "just kidding" remarks that carry hidden stings.

True humor doesn't wound. It lifts. It creates laughter so hearty that your belly aches and your cheeks hurt. Laughter is powerful. Families who laugh together typically are the families who play together. They find joy even in tough times, building strong, lasting connections. So, lighten up, soften up, and laugh it up. The zenith of influence is laughter.

Putting It All Together

Again, please keep in mind that you don't have to utilize all eight foundational components simultaneously—though you certainly can, and over time, you likely will. These components are naturally interconnected, and when integrated, they provide remarkable stability, wisdom, and contentment. Yet, each component is a powerhouse. I encourage you to explore each component individually to fully appreciate its unique strengths and experience the rewards it offers.

When I coach clients, I often ask which of the Magnificent 8 resonates with them the most. Which components do they instinctively gravitate toward? I encourage them to start with those as they are more likely to implement them quickly and effectively.

As clients progress, they begin to recognize the intrinsic connections among the eight components. The rewards of embodying the Magnificent 8 are truly nothing shy of transformative. You'll find yourself becoming a lifelong believer. It shapes your way of thinking, feeling, acting, and living magnificently.

The Magnificent 8

For fun, let me show you how the M8 can support your family traditions by creating a New Year's activity called Family Fun for Everyone. Before my client presented this idea to his family, I guided him through the Magnificent 8.

1. **Put Your Oxygen Mask on First.** He began by metaphorically putting on his oxygen mask and practicing the 4-7-8 breathing technique. This calmed both his mind and body, providing the clarity needed to grasp his new idea fully before sharing it with his family. By taking a moment to breathe, he grounded himself, allowing him to visualize his idea and articulate his thoughts more effectively rather than winging it and sharing it prematurely.
2. **Begin with the End in Mind.** Next, he envisioned the goal of Family Fun for Everyone. What outcome was he aiming for? This tool helped him get clear on his goals and objectives: creating family closeness and fun traditions and spending quality time together to build lasting memories. With a clear vision of his goals, he could see the bigger picture, which allowed him to stay on the right path to achieve his desired outcome.
3. **If It Is to Be, It Is Up to Me.** He activated the ten most powerful two-letter words: "If It Is to Be, It Is Up to Me," within him. He recognized that if this new family tradition was going to be a thing, it depended on him and his leadership. He couldn't sit on the sidelines wishing and waiting for others to read his mind and take the initiative. If this was going to happen, it was up to him. The quality of the experience would reflect the quality of his leadership.
4. **Desire and Discipline: The Dynamic Duo.** He knew that Family Fun for Everyone would die on the vine if his desire and interest were insincere and if his discipline was flatlined. Desire and discipline had to ride shotgun to ensure his plan (again) didn't end up in the graveyard of good ideas. By fueling his desire and committing to discipline, he could

transform this idea into a lasting and enjoyable family tradition.
5. **The 4 A's.** He then ran his idea through the 4 A's:
   - **Awareness.** He became aware of his previous lack of leadership and involvement in family traditions.
   - **Acknowledge.** He acknowledged he had been a passive observer in planning family activities, recognizing the need for great improvement.
   - **Assess.** He assessed ways to make "Family Fun for Everyone" a positive and enjoyable tradition while identifying potential obstacles that could derail his efforts.
   - **Action.** After laying out the positives and negatives, he took decisive action to implement the elements that would contribute to the success of this newfound activity. And voilà! A well-thought-out plan for Family Fun for Everyone was born.
6. **JED is Dead.** He knew there could be a million justifications, excuses, or defenses he could use on why this new tradition wouldn't stick. JEDing reveals your insecurities and fears by creating distraction, procrastination, or postponement of action. He stopped the unhelpful noise in his head saying why he shouldn't do this, and he remembered the goal, the outcome he desired, and the purpose of it.
7. **Pain of Regret or Pain of Discipline.** If he chose not to commit to this new family tradition, he knew the regret would haunt him. He'd feel like an ineffective leader who failed to launch, and he would sacrifice the memories and closeness he could have created with his family. If he chose discipline and saw it through, he would feel proud of himself, contribute strength to his family's foundation, and feel empowered that he created an incredible family event that could turn into a lifelong family tradition.
8. **Humor.** He understood that humor could be a powerful tool to diffuse any potential resistance to his new family activity.

The Magnificent 8

His family could be a tough crowd and might try to shoot down his idea. By infusing levity and laughter into his delivery, he made the idea humorous and engaging. When in doubt, he knew the value of a good laugh.

Boom! That's how the M8 rolls! It provides you with a solid foundation and infrastructure. It's more than just a method; it's a way of thinking, feeling, doing, and being.

You're Too Smart to Be This Foolish

You already know that developing a new skill, habit, or mindset requires commitment, consistency, and time. The reward? Transformation: a better you and a better life. The same can be said for the M8. The M8 isn't a magic seed. Instead, think of it like planting a garden. You wouldn't expect to toss seeds into your backyard and harvest them the next day. A healthy garden demands constant care throughout the entire process. The seeds need fertile soil, water, sunlight, shade, and ongoing attention to flourish. And just like your garden, you, too, need nurturing. You are a lifelong student in the classroom of life, an ever-evolving being.

Consistency is key. If you neglect your garden, weeds will take over, pests will invade, and what once held potential is left in shambles. These tools are meant to be lived every day, not as a part-time gig. A thriving life is a full-time commitment. The only way to achieve results is through your desire and discipline. Remember, your direction in life is far more important than your speed. Those who lean into their lives facing forward and who embrace each moment as an opportunity to learn find joy in the journey. We excel at what we practice repeatedly, whether it's positive or negative. Your life and your family are yours to enhance. How do you want to be remembered? What story do you want your family to tell?

Throughout this book, you'll see how the M8 weaves into every aspect of life, making everything not just better but truly *magnificent*!

Chapter 3
Understanding the Young Brain

> *"Welcome to the human brain, the cathedral of complexity."*
> ~Peter Coveney and Roger Highfield[5]

Becoming a better parent requires you to understand the most crucial part of your child: their brain. Research shows that a child's brain continues to develop well into their mid-to-late twenties.[6] By recognizing which stage of development your child's command center is in, you'll be better equipped to set realistic expectations, interpret their behavior, and become a more effective, connected parent.

Many parents miss the mark in understanding what's happening with their children. Instead of tuning into the unique neurological development of their child, they often rely on their own set of beliefs and expectations to make assumptions. While it's easy to fall back on what we think we know, advancements in neuroscience continuously reveal the complexities of the brain and remind us that

---

[5] Peter Coveney and Roger Highfield, *Frontiers of Complexity: The Search for Order in a Chaotic World,* New York: Fawcett Columbine, 1995.
[6] MIT, Youth Adult Development Project, Dr. Rae Simpson
https://hr.mit.edu/static/worklife/youngadult/contact.html

there's always more to learn—mind-blowing data! This is why it's important to stay informed about the brain's development, particularly during your children's formative years.

Understanding the young brain can provide invaluable insights into how to best support your child, which can revolutionize your relationship with them. If you're unaware of the limitations imposed by your child's still-developing neurological wiring, you risk setting them up for failure, which can strain your relationship and poison their self-esteem. Think of it this way: when you discover that your child has, let's say allergies or asthma, you would immediately take action to learn as much as possible on what protocols you'd need to have in place, what to expect, and how to handle difficult scenarios when things go awry. The same principle applies to their neurological development. For example, if your child struggles in school or with social connections, it's often due to the interplay between their brain's development and the flood of hormones during adolescence. Before jumping to conclusions and hiring tutors or labeling your child as "socially awkward," take the time to educate yourself on what is happening during this developmental stage. There's a reason adolescence can feel so challenging: a surge of neurological, biological, and hormonal changes is underway. In time, that surge will mellow out.

Understanding the adolescent brain is just one piece of the puzzle. Equally important is the environment in which the brain develops, especially the quality of thoughts swirling in their minds. This is where the sentiment, "What you think, you become," attributed to Buddha, offers powerful insight into how our mental chatter can shape our everyday lives. Often, a surprising number of these thoughts are negative and are the same ruminations repeated over and over. Simple phrases like "I dread Mondays," "I hate cloudy days," "Where are my stupid keys?" or "Traffic is a nightmare" might seem like harmless gripes, but they carry a negative energy that affects our mental state.

The fantastic news is that we have the power to rewire our thought patterns and create new, more positive ones that lead to

Understanding the Young Brain

more satisfying outcomes and better attitudes. It's truly remarkable how we can train our brains to work in our favor. Since we are creatures of habit, both the good and the bad, it's essential to perform quality control on our thoughts. Doing so gives us full control and ownership of the quality of our lives. The choice is always ours.

Our habits determine our future. Look at the habits of your brain chatter; it matters! On the topic of creating positive and productive patterns in the brain, consider incorporating a family mantra into your daily routine. That can be a powerful tool for shaping your family's thought patterns. Even if it feels silly, cheesy, or a bit forced at first, do it anyway. A mantra brings fun, empowerment, and a stronger sense of cohesion to your tribe.

Work together as a family to choose mantras that resonate with everyone. Use them regularly, whether before school, a sports game, a recital, or an important interview. These phrases can strengthen your family's foundation, reinforce your relationships, and boost your children's confidence. For instance, if you regularly tell your child, "Make it a great day!" or "Let's do this thing!" or "Never quit!" their brain will start to internalize these messages. When faced with challenges, their brain will naturally recall these mantras, which will keep them empowered or help them navigate obstacles with confidence.

In my family, we have a slew of sayings passed down through four generations. Some are hilarious, some are powerful, and some don't make much sense, yet we say them anyway for a good laugh. It's these meaningful and quirky mantras that make our family, well, us.

As parents, you have a unique opportunity to shape your children's thought patterns, which will empower them to make their brains allies rather than adversaries. Make no mistake: the brain can be bossy and stubborn, but it's also trainable. By helping them quiet their minds and take charge of their thoughts, you guide them toward forging productive pathways that will benefit them for a lifetime. And those mighty mantras? They not only nurture healthy new thought patterns but also strengthen the bond of family camaraderie.

Quick reminder: training our brain isn't a weekend project; it's a daily commitment and a lifelong investment. Keep those expectations in alignment with reality. Speaking of expectations, let's take it a step further...

Expectations, Resetting the Bar

Every parent I've coached has faced a common challenge, and that is many of their expectations don't align with their child's biological and neurological development. In today's fast-paced world, fear-based parenting often leads to unrealistic, and sometimes impossible, expectations. But here's the truth we can't forget: Every child gets one childhood; there are no do-overs. Ideally, it should be a time of unstructured play, creativity, exploration, and the freedom to simply be. Childhood should overflow with laughter, little adventures, wild curiosities, imaginative thoughts, and quiet moments to dream.

Today's children often face an uphill battle of relentless achievement, competition, and comparison. Their days are packed with activities—tutors, therapy, extra classes, volunteering, sports, clubs, music lessons—all aimed at keeping them ahead of the pack. This pressure begins as early as kindergarten, fostering an anxious environment that impacts their mental, emotional, and physical well-being. The result? Alarming rates of anxiety, depression, and stress-related disorders among today's youth. And the responsibility for change lies with us—the adults, the leaders of our homes, communities, and society.

Consider how many adults spend their lives in therapy, trying to heal from childhood wounds. Much of their pain stems from the expectations and dysfunctions passed down from their parents. As we discussed in Chapter 1, it's all connected to the many layers of who you are, your family's culture, and the ecosystem you've created. What happens at home doesn't stay at home. It stays with them,

Understanding the Young Brain

either weakening or strengthening them as they move forward in life.

It's time to break these unhealthy cycles. In today's world, we're inundated with 24/7 podcasts, social media, YouTube channels, books, motivational apps, and Netflix docuseries on how to be better parents and raise happier children. There's no shortage of helpful information. If anything, we're oversaturated with it. So, the real question is: Are you ready to take the knowledge at your fingertips and put it into action?

As the leader of your family, are you ready to take responsibility, let go of your insecurities, stop comparing your family to others, and focus on what truly matters within your family? If so, one of the most impactful changes you can make is rethinking and resetting the expectations you have for your children. Often, these expectations can unintentionally set them up for struggle because they don't align with where your children are developmentally. Recognizing this fact is a powerful first step toward creating a healthy, nurturing environment that honors their abilities and deepens your connection.

It's never too late to reset, rethink, and restart. This relentless wave of expectations starts as early as kindergarten and only intensifies. By high school, your child is juggling hours of homework, projects, sports, music lessons, tutoring, community service, and college prep, while also expected to maintain emotional intelligence, get enough sleep, stay motivated, make wise decisions, and navigate social media 24/7. Every time I go over that list, I cringe.

If you believe that setting the bar impossibly high will make your child more capable, competent, and confident, I challenge you to research the state of our youth's mental health. The reality is that we're creating a generation of exhausted, anxious, fearful, and burned-out young people. As a society, we've created this imbalance, or what I call being "overfed and undernourished." Our kids are overfed with unrealistic expectations and undernourished with what they truly need: good health, strong values, social connections, meaningful relationships, and time to enjoy the simple things in life.

Parents, Grow Up!

But really, I'm not talking about lowering the bar. I'm talking about understanding that your child's brain is still under construction. I often tell the parents I coach, "It's like expecting a kindergartener to understand algebra when they've just started to learn how to count."

When you understand the reality of their brain development, you can set realistic expectations that they're capable of achieving. This builds their confidence through competence and empowers them to exceed those expectations in a healthy, balanced way.

A great way to revisit your expectations is to start by listing all the ones you currently have for your kids. Think about their self-care, household responsibilities, social interactions, academics, extracurricular activities, nutrition, sleep, and long-term goals. You might be surprised by how many expectations you've set and how many may not align with your child's age or developmental stage.

As you create this list, prioritize expectations that nurture essential qualities like self-care, competence, independence, interpersonal skills, and mastery of life's basics. These are the building blocks of a healthy, fulfilling life. Remember, the ultimate goal is to prepare them for the real world, which extends far beyond the family home or the classroom. Stay focused on what truly matters!

An effective way to apply one of the M8 components is by reviewing your expectations through the 4 A's:

1. **Awareness.** Recognize your unrealistic expectations. (We all have them!)
2. **Acknowledge.** Admit your expectations are out of balance. (This makes change possible!)
3. **Assess.** Determine which expectations are sensible and which are unreasonable. (Provides clarity on what works and what doesn't)
4. **Action.** Move forward with realistic expectations. (Positive path illuminated!)

Understanding the Young Brain

Why Our Youth Are Struggling—and How We Can Help

Our youth are facing unprecedented challenges, and the data is alarming. But we don't need statistics to see what's happening. We need to open our eyes to see what's really happening and take action to right the wrongs—or, at the very least, take steps in the right direction.

From the widespread availability of marijuana and nicotine products that are in the hands of our middle schoolers to the omnipresence of smartphones, social media, and video games, our modern ecosystem has become a breeding ground for mental health issues. Instead of creating environments that fortify and empower our young people, we've built one that weakens and even sickens them.

To truly understand the depth and impact of anxiety on today's youth, I highly recommend Jonathan Haidt's book, *The Anxious Generation*. It's a vital resource that sheds light on the crisis we're facing. Anxiety levels among our children have escalated to beyond alarming. They've become debilitating and life-threatening. This crisis is fueled by a society that prioritizes profit over well-being, and it demands our immediate attention. As parents, we have the power to make a difference, starting in our own homes. Changing this toxic ecosystem requires collective effort—doing nothing isn't an option. Far too many young people are caught in a vicious cycle where anxiety is normalized, overprotection becomes the default, and medication is often seen as the only answer. They're yearning for real connection and purpose in a world that feels increasingly untethered and disconnected. But it doesn't have to stay this way. The current system—driven by money, power, and profit—profits from their pain. It's time to break this cycle and create a healthier path forward.

We have both the responsibility and the power to create a healthier, more enriching world for our kids. The good news? We can pivot now and shape an ecosystem that truly supports them, starting with the tech in their hands, as well as ours.

Parents, Grow Up!

Learning to tame the tech beast isn't just a good idea; it's a critical life skill in this hyper-connected virtual world. True wellness, for both you and your children, depends on understanding the dangers of tech and then taking action for healthy habits to form. It requires M8 #4, Desire and Discipline: The Dynamic Duo.

Check Tech: Reclaim Your Time and Energy

To help my clients gain insight into their relationship with technology, I developed a simple and effective exercise called "Check Tech." This exercise provides a clear picture of how you spend your time and energy online and the emotional impact it has on you.

Remember, parents, telling is not teaching; it's about showing them. Lead by example and make this a family activity. Every few months, I do a Check Tech to reflect on my own habits. Sometimes, I'm absolutely disgusted by how much my usage has spiked, often mirroring how I felt during those times—irritable, unproductive, and exhausted. Other times, I'm gleeful of the boundaries I've set, reaping the benefits of my discipline of more energy and productivity, a better mood, and extra time. It's a great way to stay mindful and accountable.

Here's how it works:

1. **List Your Apps.** In the first column, write down all the apps you use daily on your devices. For example: texting, emailing, Google searches, YouTube, social media, games, shopping, podcasts, etc.
2. **Track Your Time.** In the second column, note how much time you spend on each one. If you use an iPhone, check the Screen Time feature in your settings to get accurate data. For instance:
   - **Texting.** Checked throughout the day, averaging ninety-three pickups and thirty-nine minutes of use daily.
   - **Emailing.** Checked four times a day, totaling three hours.
   - **Google.** Checked twenty-three times a day, totaling ninety minutes.

Understanding the Young Brain

- **YouTube.** Watched three times a day, totaling two hours.
- **Instagram.** Checked sixteen times a day, totaling four hours.

3. **Reflect on Your Feelings.** In the final column, jot down how each activity makes you feel:
   - **Texting.** I feel like I'm always "on" with zero downtime.
   - **Emailing.** It makes me anxious. "Did I respond? Did I get a response?" It feels never-ending.
   - **Google.** It can be both distracting and useful but often leads to procrastination.
   - **YouTube.** While satisfying for learning, it's easy to lose hours. I often feel irritated and regretful for wasting time.
   - **Instagram.** Numbing, a time-suck that leads to FOMO. I feel angry and disgusted with myself for wasting time.
   - **Shopping Sites.** Initially exciting but ultimately irritating for spending money on things I don't need. A costly distraction.

This exercise isn't just about recognizing the problem; it's the first step toward cultivating a more mindful and balanced relationship with technology. By being honest and leading by example, we can equip our children with the skills they need to thrive in this digital age without being controlled by it. Technology is here to stay, and it will continue to advance and expand. It's up to us to establish healthy boundaries for a healthy relationship with tech.

Have you ever really stopped to examine your relationship with technology? Or do you just assume, "I've got this," only to find yourself doom-scrolling at 2 a.m., wondering why you spent $300 on a tarot reading and bought another juicer when you already have one collecting dust?

The Check Tech exercise uncovers where your time goes, how it affects you, and what it truly costs. You might think, "I'm on social media for three hours a day? No wonder I feel frustrated and unproductive." It's a tough pill to swallow, but recognizing the problem is the first step toward breaking free. It takes courage, but that same courage lets you take back your power and use technology in ways that support and serve you.

And it's not just about you. Your tech habits affect your entire family's mood and dynamic. Check Tech is a crucial first step to healthier changes, opening the door to essential conversations and helping you forge a new relationship with technology based on balance, boundaries, and respect.

As the leader of your family, it's up to you to chart the course. After you've done Check Tech, encourage everyone else to do the same. Now's the time to see how technology shapes mood, energy, and time for the whole family. Ask which apps fuel creativity and which ones leave everyone drained. Notice if weekends vanish into Netflix marathons and YouTube spirals instead of outdoor adventures, social get-togethers, or community involvement.

Here's a quick fix: carve out intentional, tech-free moments for everyone, starting with meals and outdoor activities. Nobody needs a screen during these times. Be fully present. Make mealtime a device-free zone, and reclaim that space for real conversations. And while it's tempting to snap every sunset on a hike, try living the moment instead of posting it.

Small but deliberate shifts like these can narrow the gap between distraction and connection. Let's face it: Distraction is the enemy of meaningful relationships, and technology is the biggest distraction of our era. How can we deepen our bonds when we're constantly pulled away by screens? And how can our kids experience real connection if their strongest connection is to a digital device?

Expect pushback from your kids, possibly even withdrawal symptoms for a week or two. Phones, laptops, and video games are addictive, and we've all helped create this environment. Instead of blaming others, remember: we're in it together. You're the family leader, so lead well. Don't abandon this mission just because of turbulence or tantrums.

This is the perfect time to use the Magnificent 8 to give you clarity, accountability, and the wisdom to make intentional decisions that lead to a more balanced, fulfilling life. You don't have to use all eight

Understanding the Young Brain

components; just choose what best supports you and your family's healthy tech boundaries.

Here's how the M8 can help:

1. **Put Your Oxygen Mask on First.** Before diving into tough family conversations, ground yourself. Practice a few calming breaths (like 4-7-8) to settle your mind and speak with ease.
2. **Begin with the End in Mind.** Start each discussion with a clear goal. Knowing your desired outcome keeps you focused and on track.
3. **If It Is to Be, It Is up to Me.** You have more power than you realize. Use it to set healthy tech boundaries and empower your family.
4. **Desire and Discipline.** Both are essential. Without desire, your words fall flat; without discipline, nothing sticks.
5. **The 4 A's.** First, be aware of any tech imbalance. Next, acknowledge it and admit there's room for improvement. Then, assess what's working well and what isn't. Finally, take action. Build on what works and eliminate what doesn't.
6. **Pain of Regret or Pain of Discipline.** Will you let an unhealthy tech relationship grow into regret, or take the disciplined approach and create a better path?
7. **JED is Dead.** Watch for justifying, excusing, or defending, habits that keep you from doing the tough but necessary work.
8. **Humor.** Lighten the mood with humor to create a space where everyone can speak and be heard (and maybe even enjoy the conversation).

Let the M8 strengthen who you are and how you lead. Trust me, it works every time. And speaking of trust, let's explore why it's the bedrock of family relationships.

Chapter 4
In Family We Trust

"Trust is the oxygen to all relationships."
~Jill Avery

In this chapter, we'll take a closer look at the subtle, often elusive elements of trust. You'll learn how to build, nurture, and deepen trust within your family, starting by understanding its intangible, intricate layers. Trust is very complex; it is woven into our words and actions, quietly influencing and shaping our relationships.

As we unpack these ideas, it's natural to feel a bit overwhelmed. This is a challenging territory, but since trust is the most precious thing in a family, it deserves the spotlight. So, take it one concept at a time.

Ahead, you'll find new ways of thinking to help shift your mindset and build deeper trust within your family. Think of these ideas as your trust toolkit filled with strategies, methods, and practices. Start with one concept at a time, digest it, and then put it into action. Some ideas will resonate more than others, and that's perfectly okay. Begin with those. Just promise yourself to be brave enough to try each one. These tools are timeless, and both you and your family relationships are worth the investment.

Because repetition and consistency are required for creating habits, here comes yet another big, fat reminder: no fairy godmother is waving her wand to create the family and life you want (I checked). Wellness, health, and harmony in any relationship require two things: desire and discipline.

Trust me (yes, pun fully intended!), here again, there are only three reasons why these tools won't work for you:

1. You don't believe in them.
2. You don't apply them.
3. You don't stay consistent and committed to using them.

Let's first start with Merriam-Webster's definition of trust: "Assured reliance on the character, ability, strength, or truth of someone or something."[7] Sounds good enough, but trust goes far beyond a tidy, dictionary definition. It's the oxygen of relationships, especially within a family.

Trust doesn't just exist because we are family; it's something we carefully grow over time. It grows through shared experiences, how we treat each other, the words we choose (because words do matter), and, ultimately, the actions we take. Trust is something we nurture every single day. There's no done-and-dusted moment. It's like the garden analogy; it takes great care, effort, attention, and consistent tending to keep it healthy and thriving. The same goes for trust. It is a daily commitment to our character, values, self-worth, and the relationships we value.

Being the leader of your family, you've automatically inherited the noble (and often exasperating) role of Chief Trust Officer. It's your responsibility to cultivate an environment where trust is built and honored according to how each family member perceives it.

So, how do we start turning trust into something a little more concrete? Easy: start with some good old-fashioned, open, honest conversations. Here's a great jumping-off point: Create a comfortable

---

[7] *Merriam-Webster's Unabridged Dictionary*, s.v. "trust," accessed 2024, https://unabridged.merriam-webster.com/unabridged/trust.

environment (phones set aside and out of sight) and ask your family some of these questions to spark a discussion about trust:

- How do you define trust?
- Do you feel you have trust in each other?
- Do you consider yourself a trusting person?
- Do you see yourself as trustworthy?
- How do you rebuild trust once it's been broken?

These questions may ignite an enlightening conversation, but they are also your fast track to building a stronger family trust structure. And here's a little secret: magic happens when you listen—not the distracted, going-through-the-motions type of listening, but the wholehearted, I'm-here-and-am-all-ears kind. The parents I coach often tell me how surprised they are by how insightful and enjoyable these conversations turn out to be. These discussions give parents a chance to see how their kids perceive trust on different levels, while also providing an opportunity to share their own perspectives. These open and thoughtful conversations are what contribute to your family's foundation of trust.

What's wonderful about these open, genuine conversations is that they capture the actual essence of trust itself: valuing, respecting, and honoring each other's perspectives, even when they differ. These are the beautiful, powerful intangibles of trust that keep you connected and woven together like a cozy blanket.

Take these wise words attributed to Walt Whitman, "Be curious, not judgmental," and remember them before you respond. Curiosity is one of the most effective tools in your trust-building toolkit. When trust in a family falters, so do the bonds that hold the family together—closeness, stability, and a sense of safety.

Now, let's slide into one of the most elusive and profound aspects of trust, the piece that affects your children's self-worth and shapes their lives: your belief in them.

Trust and Belief: Two Sides of the Same Coin

Trust and belief are deeply intertwined and form one of the most valuable gifts you can offer your children. Believing in your children means trusting their abilities, resilience, and potential, while truly trusting them means having faith in their capacity to face challenges and thrive.

It's not just about confidence in their ability to achieve specific goals, such as academic success, sports trophies, or landing a job. It's about trusting and believing that, at their core, they already possess everything they need to create a meaningful and fulfilling life. Together, trust and belief form the foundation of confidence and support, empowering your kids to reach their full potential.

When parents don't believe in their children, or when children don't feel that belief, they can leave deep, lasting wounds. Sure, those wounds might scab over with time, but they remain vulnerable, ready to reopen during moments of insecurity.

Your trust and belief in your children are essential to their well-being, especially during life's inevitable rough patches when they experience self-doubt, heartbreaks, failures, and fears. At times, they'll need to borrow your belief in them to navigate these challenges. When you trust your children, you instill in them the confidence to trust themselves, step outside their comfort zones, and face life head-on. As a parent, one of your most inspiring and enchanting abilities is to ignite the spark of self-belief in your child. How? By demonstrating your belief in them, day after day, moment by moment. They'll feel it and think: *If my parents believe I'm capable, strong, or smart enough, then I must be!* Until they find that belief within themselves, let them borrow yours.

If you want a deep, meaningful connection with your children, one built on trust and a strong bond, they need to feel that you believe in them. You don't have to agree with every decision they make, but they must know you have faith in their ability to figure things out and find their way.

In Family We Trust

Self-identity is arguably the most impactful belief system we carry. How we defined ourselves as children often mirrored how our parents defined us. Kids naturally believe what their parents say; after all, we are supposed to be their most trusted leaders. That is why it's so important to be mindful and intentional with your opinions, beliefs, and words. Think back to your childhood. How would it have felt to carry your parents' belief in your heart? Remember, neither children nor parents need to have everything figured out to move in the right direction. Growth and learning are never linear; trusting and believing in the process is what truly matters.

While actions may speak louder than words, never underestimate the power of what you say. Words can either wound or uplift, and both effects can last a lifetime. The words you choose during your child's formative years often become monuments in their minds, etched into their self-identity. You may forget what you said; you may not even believe you said it. But your children, whether they're still young or already adults, may have attached their sense of self to those words. It's not about blaming yourself but about recognizing the weight and responsibility of your words so you speak with care.

Your children start out trusting you, and they will take your words to heart. But as they grow, they will start to question and challenge everything. Your trust will need to be earned and sometimes repaired.

As a parent, I've had moments of reckoning when my now-adult children shared with me the words I spoke during their childhood. To my horror, some of those words, spoken in moments I've long forgotten, took root in their subconscious and influenced their self-worth. Because they trusted me—their mom, their biggest fan—why wouldn't they believe what I said? If we hadn't discussed the power of words, I would never have known the lasting impact, and those words might have continued to fester inside them. As parents, we hold tremendous power, and with that power comes great responsibility. Be brave, be vulnerable, and ask your kids if they are carrying anything from past conversations that might still affect them. It's essential to have these conversations sooner rather than later to prevent any potential harm to their self-worth. Open up the dialogue to highlight the importance of checking in with each other and recognizing how things can be misinterpreted. This will encourage your kids to be more open about their thoughts and feelings, especially during conversations that could be misinterpreted or lead to misunderstandings. It's a fantastic opportunity to address issues before they take root in their subconscious.

When our children trust us, trust our words and our belief in them, they begin to trust themselves. This self-trust allows them to believe in their own abilities, take responsibility for their actions, and internalize one of the most valuable lessons you can teach, which is that life is an inside job. Fulfillment doesn't come from the outside; it's something we create within. From a young age, help them understand that their greatest investment is in their own wellness and wholeness. Teach them to value the essentials of self-love, self-care, self-worth, self-confidence, self-sufficiency, and self-competence.

When we teach our children to focus on strengthening those core self-essentials, we empower our children to grow into self-confident and reliant adults capable of creating meaningful lives. However, neglecting to teach responsibility and accountability—whether it's for themselves, their pets, their homes, or their relationships—risks what is called "learned helplessness," which can spiral into deeply seeded insecurity and anxiety. The term "enabler" is often used to describe this kind of parenting. But in truth, it goes beyond enabling; it disables the child's ability to navigate life on their own. It's a double-edged sword that cuts away at both their competence and confidence.

These elements of trust—belief and the understanding that life is an inside job—may seem elusive, but they are fundamental to both the strength of your relationship with your kids and the health of their self-worth.

Now, let's move on to one of the touchiest topics for parents.

No One, I Mean, *No One*, Likes a Know-It-All

After decades of working with parents and coaching youth, I've learned that one of the most effective ways to build trust is to admit that you don't know it all. Show your kids that you are a lifelong learner, are open to new ideas, and want to evolve. You'd be surprised how many kids believe their parents would rather be right than be open—open to listening, to learning, to changing. Let's face it: No one likes a know-it-all. When parents act like they have all the answers simply because they're parents, they undermine trust, silence their kids' thoughts and feelings, and create a deep divide.

If you're holding onto the idea that you're the expert just because you're the parent, your kids might start thinking you don't trust their thoughts, ideas, or abilities. And let's be honest: Who wants to feel like they're always being second-guessed? Around the age of ten, kids begin to step out of the I'll-do-what-you-say phase and into the Why-should-I? phase. They start pushing back, questioning what you say and do. This is expected, natural, and—believe it or not—welcomed. It's called maturing, growing up. They are craving an increasing amount of independence in their thinking, feeling, and doing.

Remember one of M8's timeless tools: *Begin with the End in Mind*. So, what's the goal here? The answer's pretty straightforward: to raise healthy, self-competent, kind, and independent adults. Yes, kids grow up, and the aim is to ensure they become self-reliant, confident, and healthy adults. Just keep in mind that both you and your children will continue to evolve, as individuals and as a family, throughout your lives.

So, take a deep breath, ride the wave, and stay open, flexible, adaptable, and curious. One of my all-time favorite quotes that I love sharing with my clients comes from Frederick W. Robertson: "The true aim of everyone who aspires to be a teacher should be not to impart their own opinions but to kindle minds."[8] As a parent, your greatest asset is your willingness to learn right alongside your kids. Let them know they're one of your greatest teachers. Because, honestly, families that learn together absolutely grow together. So, lighten up and enjoy the ride!

Trust is built when your words match your actions. When you lead by example, your kids naturally follow. But if you're stuck in that know-it-all mindset, it becomes a huge liability when building trust. You've seen it before, right? We all know someone who's always telling and instructing but never actually practicing what they preach. And what do we do? We don't usually confront them; we just quietly note, "Yep! No trust here. Feels like a one-way street." Trust isn't something you can demand or expect; it's something you earn day by day, with effort, time, and genuine care, just like caring for your garden. Without that alignment between what you say and what you do, trust slowly withers away—just as the weeds take over.

Now that you have a deeper understanding of the power of trust, let's take the next step and explore additional ways to strengthen trust within your family.

---

[8] Robertson, Frederick William. Two Lectures on the Influence of Poetry on the Working Classes, Delivered Before the Members of the Mechanic's Institution, February, 1852. United Kingdom: King, 1852.

Chapter 5
Mindset Shifts for Mastering Your Response + Abilities

"A kind word can change someone's day, a thoughtful response can change someone's life."

In this chapter, we focus on the profound responsibility parents have in building and strengthening trust with their kids. As I often emphasize throughout this book: "With enormous power comes enormous responsibility," and as parents, our "response + abilities" lie at the heart of this responsibility. By shifting our mindset, we pave the way for meaningful changes in our behavior, building the foundation for lasting trust and strong, wonderful relationships with our kids.

Improving how we communicate with our kids begins with reexamining how we think. Consider the well-known quote often attributed to Albert Einstein: "Insanity is doing the same thing over and over and expecting different results." Now, let's reframe it: *Insanity is communicating the same way over and over and expecting different results.*

Building trust isn't just about what you say; it's about making sure your actions back it up. Lip service is a trust detonator. When your words are hollow, trust falters—not because your kids choose not to trust you but because that's simply how trust works. This principle extends beyond parenting. It applies to any relationship. To be a trustworthy and influential leader in your child's life, your words and actions must be a tight partnership—like PB & J or biscuits and gravy. Mastering your ability to respond requires an intentional shift in mindset in how you think, what you think, and why. In this chapter and the next, I'll introduce some new mindsets and actionable strategies to help you create meaningful, lasting change. It all starts with how you think and how you choose to respond.

Let's begin by exploring some of the most effective mindset shifts to help you rethink your approach and respond more productively. These shifts create new ways of thinking and support actions that strengthen trust with your kids. Even small shifts can lead to pivotal change.

Go-To-Responses Supported by the M8

In those inevitable heated conversations with our kids, how we respond can make all the difference. When emotions run high and hijack our ability to think clearly, it's easy to let frustration take over. But when heated reactions take the wheel, trust gets kicked to the trunk and is often replaced by fear, tears, or shutdown.

Speaking from (lots of) experience, when I allowed my emotions to take over with my kids, it robbed me of the chance to understand, teach, or listen. All they remembered was my emotional volcanic eruption, an outpouring of emotional lava, leaving them feeling scared, withdrawn, and less trusting of me.

So yes, I completely understand. I totally get it. It's hard not to react. It can even feel impossible to suppress, just like one of the crazy sneezes that come out of nowhere. I used to be the Queen of Sarcasm. It felt like my native tongue. My responses were quick, clever, biting, and, most often, unfair.

Back then, I would JED (Hello M8 #7 JED—Justify, Excuse, and Defend) my sarcastic quips so I didn't feel like such a punitive and

Mindset Shifts for Mastering Your Response + Abilities

petty mom. As my Southern grandmother used to say, "Pretty is as pretty does." In other words, I might've appeared to be a kind mom, but my sarcasm revealed the ugly truth. Shifting my mindset to silence my sarcasm and respond more thoughtfully took time, but the rewards have been priceless. Responses delivered with care are felt instantly, creating a boomerang effect that sends that care right back.

What helped me make this mindset shift was the M8. To break my habit of sarcastic, impulsive responses, I leaned on these:

1. **Put Your Oxygen Mask on First.** Taking a pause, breathing, and getting grounded make impulsiveness nearly impossible.
6. **Pain of Regret or Pain of Discipline.** Thinking through my choices and their outcomes brought clarity and helped me make wiser decisions.

Remember, we improve with practice. Commit to mastering your ability to respond thoughtfully and let the M8 support your mindset shift. Here are a few go-to responses to keep handy for managing heated conversations:

- "I know I have a lot to learn, especially from you." (For when you just need to shut your pie-hole and listen.)
- "Whatever it takes, you can count on me." (For validating that no matter what, even if you disagree, you're here to stay.)
- "Are you open to my perspective?" (For respecting their thoughts by really listening before offering your own.)

Having go-to responses in your back pocket strengthens your response + abilities. They give you the space to pause and approach situations more thoughtfully. This practice fosters patience—an invaluable virtue, especially during those years when your teen's determination feels like it's on steroids, rebelling against almost everything (even the way you breathe).

Mastering the art of responding starts with muzzling the impulse to react. Only then can you focus on addressing your child's behavior, not just the outcomes of that behavior. Stay grounded in leading by example: show your ability to listen, remain open to understanding, and stay calm. It's an invaluable skill and creates a lasting impact!

Patience + Time

Patience is one of the toughest parts of parenting—patience of any kind. The type of patience I'm talking about here is the kind that requires time, the patience to see things through and wait for the fruits of your labor to flourish. It's about keeping the big picture in focus and holding onto the mindset of beginning with the end in mind (M8 #2), even when frustration, disappointment, or impatience threatens to take over.

Building a close family, raising healthy and whole kids, nurturing loving and enjoyable relationships, and establishing a foundation of solid trust is a journey—an ongoing process that requires unwavering commitment. It's like planting seeds: you prepare the soil, plant carefully, and then wait. You trust the process, understanding that growth takes time. But here's where it gets tricky. How often are we tempted to dig up the soil to check on the seeds? We want to make sure they've taken root or that they're at the stage we think they *should* be.

Oh boy, was I good at that—impatiently digging up my seeds, checking for progress, and doubting the process. (Patience has been, and continues to be, a lifelong practice for me.) But just like with fruit trees, you can't expect to harvest a month after planting. It takes time, sometimes years, before you see the results. Each stage of growth is essential and requires great care: tending to the soil, fertilizing, watering, weeding, and pruning.

And guess what? It's the same with our kids. Every stage matters and needs attention, care, patience, and time to grow into something strong and healthy.

This mindset shift keeps you grounded in the reality of the growth process with your uniquely individual kids. When you embrace this perspective, you're more able to welcome patience and even find joy in the journey through each stage of their development. It allows your kids the time and space they need to fully experience and grow through each phase, recognizing that every stage is formative and essential.

If, instead, parents become too focused on seeing results too soon—expecting buds to appear before their time or rushing to harvest prematurely—the growth process gets disrupted. The farmer grows frustrated and disappointed with the crop, and the crop itself stops receiving the care and attention it needs to truly thrive. Patience and trust in the process are what ensure healthy growth and a bountiful harvest, both for crops and for kids.

And here's an important side note: no matter how patient you are, your expectations need to align with what's realistically attainable. When expectations are out of reach, it can trigger a domino effect of unintended consequences. Unrealistic goals set kids up to fail and feel like failures, which erodes trust not only in you but also in themselves. It's a lose-lose situation every time.

This idea brings to mind the well-known quote: "If you judge a fish by its ability to climb a tree, it will live its whole life believing that it is stupid." The same is true for kids; they need to be nurtured and encouraged in ways that honor who they are (not who you want them to be) and not held to impossible standards that set them up for doubt and defeat.

Kindling Trust

You can't start a fire with just one big log; you need kindling to spark the flames. Trust works the same way—it's ignited by the little things. Like tending a fire, trust requires care, respect, and a steady supply of effort to keep it burning strong and bright. Just like a fire, trust can't survive on autopilot. It needs constant attention and effort to keep burning.

Having this mindset shifts your focus to the smaller things that make a big impact. Trust is built in the little, everyday actions: keeping your word, like saying, "If you finish your chores early, you can take the car to meet friends at the park"; being dependable by consistently showing up on time; and creating a home environment that feels loving, safe, and supportive. These simple actions are the kindling that keeps the fire of trust strong and steady.

It's easy to underestimate the power of these small gestures, but they are the foundation of your child's trust in you. When you consistently follow through, show up, and provide a safe space, you're telling your kids, *"I see you, I respect you, and I've got your back."* Over time, this steady effort becomes a blazing bonfire of trust that keeps your relationship warm and bright.

But remember, trust, similar to fire, can dwindle if neglected. It needs your presence, attention, and care. Small missteps—such as breaking a promise or brushing off their concerns—are like failing to add wood to keep the fire burning strong. The good news? Trust, like a fire, can be rebuilt with effort, patience, and a commitment to tending to it daily. This Kindling Trust mindset shows that mastering your response + abilities isn't just about words. It's equally about your actions. "Response" encompasses both what you say and how you follow through.

Teens, Built to Buck

As we've discussed, the teenage brain is like a house under construction; most of the wiring is operational, but some rooms aren't fully connected. From the outside, the house appears up and running, but inside, a few rooms still need finishing. It's the same with teens: the part of their brain responsible for rational, logical decisions isn't fully wired yet. That's why their thought process sometimes short-circuits, leading to impulsive choices, bucking boundaries, rebellion, and way more drama than an episode of *Love Island*. And you know what? That's completely normal. It's exactly how their brains are wired at this stage of development. I bet you've got a few tales to tell from your own teenage years to prove it! This is where a shift in mindset can work wonders. Instead of taking it personally, remind yourself that this turbulence is part of the growth process. What I often share with parents on this wild ride is that you *want* your teens to stumble, face-plant, tackle challenges, and survive a few fiascos, all while they're still under your roof.

Mindset Shifts for Mastering Your Response + Abilities

Think of your leadership and home environment as their training arena. By the time they leave the nest and step into the real world, they'll have some battle scars, learned a few lessons (fingers crossed), and gained firsthand experience with consequences. Growing up under your roof is their first crash course in how life works. They learn how to navigate bumpy times and adapt and overcome challenges. This hands-on training prepares them for greater success in adulthood. If you shelter, overprotect, or micromanage, you might as well wrap them in bubble wrap and lock them in the attic for the rest of their lives. Their wings will be clipped, and they'll never learn to fly. On the flip side, give them too much freedom and too little responsibility, and they'll be like a kite in a windstorm, darting unpredictably with no clear direction, always teetering on the edge of crashing.

The key is finding the sweet spot between these extremes. That's where the magic happens: building their self-competence and independence while nurturing their free-spirited ideas and dreams. It sounds simple, but it's incredibly hard to get right, which is why tools like the M8 are such game-changers for guiding us to shift our mindset to master our *response + abilities* and empowering us along the way.

Here's an example I often share with the parents I coach that always seems to resonate with them. Do you remember watching chicks hatch in elementary school? The eggs were kept warm under a light, simulating the heat of a mother hen. Every day, students would eagerly rush over to check on the eggs, hoping for any sign of change. Then, finally, the big moment arrived. The teacher and students gathered around the incubator, ready to witness the hatching.

As they watch, some kids start to worry. It's taking so long! They see the shells cracking as the baby chicks struggle to break free, and to them, it looks like the chicks are in trouble, maybe even in danger. As the chicks slowly push through the membrane, the children catch glimpses of their tiny heads. On the verge of tears, some pleaded with their teacher, "We need to help them! They can't breathe! They're too small and weak to get out! They're going to die if we don't do something!"

Sensing their distress, the teacher gently gathers them and explains, "We can't help the chicks break out of their shells. They need to do this on their own. This struggle is what makes them stronger and prepares them for life. As they work to break free, they're strengthening their necks, wings, and legs and learning how to use their beaks. If we intervene and make it easier for them, they won't be strong enough to hold their heads up or even stand. They need this practice to build the muscles and skills that will help them survive. The best thing we can do is let them keep working so they can grow into strong, healthy chickens."

Parents, the same goes for you: don't step in too soon. It's okay for your kids to struggle or even fail completely. Let them. These experiences are what build mental fortitude and inner strength, helping them grow into adaptable, resilient individuals. Don't break their shell for them. Instead, empower them by showing your trust in their abilities. Let them feel your confidence in their capacity to push through challenges.

The moments when our kids are struggling are some of the hardest for parents. But it's in those tough moments that the greatest opportunities arise for you to master your response. Support them, cheer them on from the sidelines, and resist the urge to step in and make things easier. These are the moments that build self-competence and confidence. It's also where parents earn their kids' trust and respect by showing they believe in their ability to handle the challenge on their own.

To prepare your kids for the real world, you need to strike a balance: give them enough space to mess up, learn adaptability, and come out stronger and more experienced. The goal is to raise capable, respectful, and confident young adults who don't just survive life but excel in building a life they love. Stay flexible in your leadership. Parenting is far from a straight path. It's an adventure full of twists, turns, setbacks, highs, lows, and discoveries. Embrace them all and appreciate and enjoy the journey.

Mindset Shifts for Mastering Your Response + Abilities

Are you starting to understand the power of shifting your mindset? That power is your mind's willingness to be open and shift. Let's keep this going ...

Behold the Behavior

When it comes to mastering your *response + abilities*, pause before jumping straight to punishment. Focus first on the behavior that needs attention and adjustment. This approach helps your kids learn from their mistakes, teaches accountability, and preserves your relationship. By leading with wisdom and composure, you model respectful and effective leadership, an invaluable lesson they'll carry forward.

Now, let me be crystal clear: I'm not referring to the dangerous and irresponsible behaviors; those just may need an iron fist. I'm referring to the behaviors most teens and young adults naturally go through as they transition into their adulthood: testing boundaries, feeling invincible, acting like a know-it-all, backtalking, swearing, lying, or throwing tantrums.

In those scenarios, think of yourself as a coach. Coaches don't immediately yank their players off the field and ban them from the game for a week just because they made a mistake. Instead, they address the problem, not the person. A coach's job is to teach, guide, and help players improve. They develop better game plans and give their players plenty of chances to practice new strategies.

If coaches kicked players off the team every time something went wrong, the players would never learn from their mistakes or learn how to improve. It's about guiding them toward a better play next time, helping them learn from poor choices, and avoiding a permanent penalty box sentence.

By approaching things this way, you're building trust and empowering them to take accountability for their actions without holding up the red card.

Let's say your teen gets caught in a lie. Instead of reacting like they've just posted that mortifying picture of you on social media

73

Parents, Grow Up!

(you know, the one they swore on their life they deleted), breathe, relax, and get your thoughts together.

Remember M8's #1 rule: Put Your Oxygen Mask on First. Approach the situation calmly (so they might actually listen) and stick to the facts, rather than blowing your top in outrage. Losing your temper does exactly what you don't want: it makes them feel your anger instead of hearing your message, causing them to withdraw, zone out, or shut down. The lesson gets lost, and instead, they learn how to tune you out, let you overheat, or retreat out of fear. Instead, draw from the mighty M8 (every one of its tools could help here), stay grounded, root yourself in wisdom, and be real. You might say something like, "Look, lying breaks trust (fact). Without trust, freedom and privileges take a hit too (consequence). It also makes people question your character (fact). I understand how things can go sideways, so let's talk about trust, how it works, and why it matters."

Responding this way creates a calm, supportive environment where your kids feel safe to open up and learn from the situation. Now, here comes the crucial part: zip it and listen. No judging, no jumping in. Just let them talk. Once they're done, ask how they'd handle the situation if they had a do-over. Again, zip it and listen. Maybe ask a few follow-up questions. Then, guide the discussion on how they're planning to rebuild trust. Again, listen. Then, when it's time, share your thoughts.

The key here is to remind them you're on the same team, working toward shared goals: restoring trust and valuing integrity. When deciding on a consequence, make sure it aligns with the lesson they need to learn, not your anger. The consequence should match the severity of the lie. For instance, lying about homework is very different from sneaking the car out for a joyride with friends. The goal is growth, not punishment. Let your family's values guide the way.

Mindset Shifts for Mastering Your Response + Abilities

The 3 C's: Calm, Clear, and Caring

Using the lying example above, once your teen has broken your trust, the path to earning it back needs to be crystal clear. And it's up to you to follow through on the consequences. If you don't, your words lose their value. Kids quickly notice when parents don't follow through, and just like that, they find the loophole. This is your golden opportunity to become masterful in your response + abilities.

Start by laying out clear expectations: what you need from them moving forward and what will happen if trust is broken again. Let them know that honesty is non-negotiable and that trust is rebuilt one brick at a time. When you respond calmly, clearly, and with care, you're not only demonstrating strong leadership and using your authority wisely, but you're also deepening that intangible bond of trust. Why? Because you're showing them a few things: 1) that you understand mistakes happen, 2) you value your relationship, and 3) you are holding them accountable for their actions.

But here's the key: don't wait for the emotional dam to break—the power of that surge is unstoppable. This is where the Three C's—Calm, Clear, and Caring—become your mantra. Staying grounded before things escalate helps you maintain composure, allowing you to teach life's most important lessons while holding your kids accountable for their words, decisions, and actions. To strengthen your Three C's mindset, remember M8 #3: If It Is to Be, It Is Up to Me. As their leader, your role is to create opportunities for them to learn, grow, and evolve into trustworthy, respectful humans, even when they have broken your trust. By staying calm, speaking clearly, and showing genuine care, you make it easier for them to listen and want to make things right. Kids learn best by doing, so resist the urge to swoop in, fix everything, or hand out punishments so heavy they overshadow the lesson. Trust in their abilities. Your kids just need the chance to prove themselves.

Parents, Grow Up!

Your Behavior Defines Your Leadership

Great parent leaders know when to step back, giving their kids the opportunity to step up, take charge, and learn how to lead themselves. Your behavior doesn't just shape your leadership; it molds the leadership qualities your kids develop. And that behavior stems directly from your mindset and your response + abilities. As the most influential leaders in your children's lives, we can't afford to act like teenagers; we've already been there and done that. If we want our kids to grow into confident, capable individuals, we need to provide them with a wide range of experiences because every experience has value.

Your behavior and leadership skills are intertwined. For example, if you haven't yet mastered managing your emotions or resisting the urge to blurt out every thought that pops into your head (trust me, I'm always working on this one), how can you expect your kids to? Your behavior speaks volumes. When you lose control, you teach your kids to either mirror your outbursts or shut down entirely. Emotional tantrums don't teach; they slam the door to your child's inner world, and for good reason. Conversely, leadership can falter when you avoid tough conversations. When your kids make poor decisions and you withdraw to dodge confrontation, you're not stepping into your role as a leader. Maybe you're afraid of their emotional reaction or worried they won't like you. But avoiding the rhino in the room doesn't make it disappear. The rhino lingers, trampling your leadership and eroding your child's respect for you. This is where a mindset shift can save the day. Pause and reflect on what you're modeling for your kids in these critical moments. How effective are your responses? Are you demonstrating behavior you'd want your kids to emulate? It's time to get real about the quality of your response + abilities. Whether your approach is explosive or avoidant, trust erodes when your kids sense inconsistency or a lack of accountability.

Here's where the M8 comes in to guide and shape your responses. Consider M8 #2: Begin with the End in Mind. Before you speak or act, ask yourself: What's my goal? What outcome am I aiming for? The goal is to lead by example to show your kids that even in difficult situations, you can create productive paths forward. That's true leadership. It builds trust and earns deep respect. Use these moments to teach and collaborate. Partner with your kids to set realistic, achievable milestones, giving them ownership of the process and motivating them to stay committed. This mindset shift enhances your leadership while empowering your kids to build the momentum they need to get back on track and stay there.

Parenting constantly reveals the kind of leader you are and the quality of your behavior. While it can feel like the hardest, most thankless job in the world, it's also the most profound and impactful role of your life. Never forget the immense power and privilege you have to shape not only your child's future but also their ability to lead themselves.

To Be Understood is Sublime

In my thirty years of work, I haven't met a single person—neither adult nor child—who hasn't resonated with this quote (attributed to Walt Whitman, whom I've crushed on for years): "It's great to be loved, but it is profound to be understood." How does it hit you?

My students often share things like, "I know my parents love me, but they don't get me," or "I'm the black sheep of the family," or "I just don't fit in." Others say, "I know I should be happy because I have a great house, a dog, and cool vacations, but they don't get me." Or "They want me to be what they think is best," and "I just fake it with my family and will be the real me when I leave the house."

Talk about the irony. As parents, we naturally want what's best for our kids. Often, our desires align: we both want them to be healthy, confident, happy, independent, and capable of building a life they're proud of. The challenge lies in defining what each of these terms means to us versus what they mean to our children. And trust me, those definitions can be so different that it may feel like you're speaking different languages. Just as we once wanted to feel prepared to launch into the world, our kids need that same readiness. And to be truly prepared, they need experience and ownership over their lives. This journey begins at home with your guidance and leadership. From the moment they were born, we've been preparing them for their lift-off—that inevitable moment when we must let go. Embracing this reality helps us see their needs and desires more clearly. At the heart of all of it lies a simple truth: they need to feel understood. What an incredible honor it is to truly know your children. What a treasure!

Take the time to understand who they are, how they think, and why they do what they do. Remember, what they share is just a moment in time, a snapshot. Their thoughts, feelings, and ideas will evolve, so don't panic. Take a breath. Be present. Be a listener. Be their support. Create a safe, trusting space where they feel free to share. When you focus on mastering your response + abilities to understand them, they'll feel it. This will deepen the trust between you and your children in a lasting, meaningful way. Trust isn't built in a single conversation; it grows through your consistent actions. Saying "I love you" is comforting, but it can feel routine.

Feeling understood, though? Whoa! Now that's next-level. It's the real effort, real care, and what love looks and feels like. It takes true presence, patience, time, and a hefty dose of genuine curiosity.

Curiosity is the how of understanding your kids. It's asking meaningful questions, wanting to know and learn more about who they are, and understanding them. Did you feel understood by your parents? If so, or if not, how did it impact you? Do you still desire to be understood by your parents? For me, the answer is a lifelong *yes*. Understanding our kids is the pinnacle of parenting.

Understanding goes deep. The deeper you go, the more you'll know. And the more you know, the better you'll understand. Go deep and relish the descent. Be curious to understand (doesn't mean agree) their thoughts, fears, ideas, dreams, and desires. Remember, you're not trying to fix, judge, or impose your ideas, but simply to understand. Resisting the urge to hijack the conversation or offer ready-made solutions is often a delicate balance. Trust the process. Don't rush. Just be present. Be kind. Be curious.

Mindset Shifts for Mastering Your Response + Abilities

This isn't about being the expert or authority. This is you genuinely striving to understand who your kids are. You don't have to agree with everything they share, but you can work to understand where they're coming from. To be understood! How profound. This is where mastering your ability to respond and listen with care becomes paramount.

The Parent Traps

Over the years, I've worked with countless parents, and most fall into one of two traps: the firehose of flattery or the firehose of fears. I'll own it. I was mostly in the flattery camp with my kids, but I definitely had my wrecking ball moments fueled by fear. When it came to flattery, I was always sincere. I adore my kids and always want them to feel it. Sometimes, my over-the-top praise landed well. But as they got older, I started noticing something. The moment I poured out my adoration, they'd repel, give a vacant stare, or flash a forced half-smile that screamed, *"OMG, Mom, stop!"* Even though my heart was in the right place, it didn't matter. The result? Total flop, fail, and disconnect.

Here's what I realized: intentions are about what *we* want—what *we* think is helpful or best—not necessarily what the other person needs. That shift in mindset was a breakthrough. I started rethinking how I connect with my kids, focusing on mastering the how, what, when, and why of my communication. The M8 has been an infallible framework on this journey, helping me navigate tricky terrain. Whether it's depressurizing my firehose of flattery or staying grounded in tough situations, the M8 provides the support and structure I need to make wiser decisions.

Here's how I applied the M8 to my firehose of flattery:

1. **Put Your Oxygen Mask on First.** Breathe, get grounded, and calm the mind and body before speaking.
2. **Begin with the End in Mind.** Keeps the bigger picture in view. What's my goal? To balance my praise in a way that honors my kids' feelings while also expressing my pride.

3. **If It Is to Be, It Is Up to Me.** I am responsible for my actions and accountable for the outcomes. Changing my mindset is up to me.
4. **Desire and Discipline.** I needed the desire to change my mindset and the discipline to stay consistent to get results.
5. **The 4 A's:**
    - **Awareness.** Recognizing my tendency to overdo flattery.
    - **Acknowledgment.** Admitting it was out of balance and needed adjustment.
    - **Assess.** The positives? Sharing my pride feels great. The negatives? My kids often find it cringeworthy, and it creates distance instead of connection.
    - **Action.** Know my audience. Subtle, sincere praise lands better than gushing.
6. **Pain of Regret or Pain of Discipline.** If I stick with my firehose of flattery, I risk damaging our relationship, a regret I can't afford. Practicing restraint and balance (discipline) allows me to honor their needs and strengthen our bond.
7. **JED is Dead (Justify, Excuse, Defend).** Sure, I could JED my over-the-top praise all day long, but that would only delay the changes I know I need to make. Owning my behavior is the first step toward meaningful progress.
8. **Humor.** Adding a touch of humor lightens the mood, with a little humor making my delivery softer and more enjoyable for everyone involved. By using the M8, I've been able to shift from overwhelming my kids with flattery to communicating in a way that strengthens our relationship. It's a powerful tool that helps me master my response + abilities, making every interaction more meaningful.

See how the M8 can support and guide you in making sound decisions for a calmer you and happier outcome?

It's easy to see why parents fall into the firehose of flattery trap. We adore our kids and want them to know just how amazing we think they are. We tell them they're the best, that they can do

Mindset Shifts for Mastering Your Response + Abilities

anything, and that the world is lucky to have them. It feels like our right, our privilege, to swoon, gush, and maybe even drool over them. But as we all have experienced, even the most well-meaning words can have unintended consequences.

When we shower our children with endless praise, we risk inflating their self-image to unhealthy levels. Some kids might start to believe they can walk on water, leading to arrogance, entitlement, and unrealistic expectations of how the world will treat them. Others may feel crushed under the weight of praise they didn't ask for, leading to insecurities, self-doubt, or imposter syndrome if they feel they can't live up to it.

Here I go again...As parents, we hold immense power. Our words and actions shape how our children view themselves and the world. This power must be used thoughtfully and with care. While it's tempting to think constant praise will fill every gap in their confidence, it can set them up for a debilitating spiral when the world doesn't reflect the same glowing feedback. Reality can strike like a punch in the gut, leaving them unprepared to cope because they were taught to walk on water, not how to swim.

So, what's the answer? Balance and moderation. Believe in your children, nurture their strengths, admire their individuality, and celebrate their wins, but also embrace their losses as valuable opportunities to build resilience and adaptability. Those essential traits come from experiencing adversity, not being shielded from it. Let them face challenges and learn to recover from life's inevitable nosedives and rogue waves. Teach them to build a healthy, realistic view of themselves and their worth, one that isn't tied solely to their achievements. Show them they're loved for who they are, not just for what they accomplish. Save the over-the-top accolades for other audiences; your kids need productive praise that prepares them for the real world.

On the flip side is the firehose of fears. This is where, in an attempt to prepare our kids for life's challenges, we bombard them with warnings: *Life will crush you if you're not the smartest or strongest. Don't trust anyone. Lower your expectations to avoid disappointment.* The intention is often to protect them, toughen them up, or prepare them for the hard knocks of life. But just like the firehose of flattery, this approach can backfire.

Some kids internalize these fear-based messages, becoming anxious, cynical, or hopeless. Others rebel, determined to prove their parents wrong. When I led with my firehose of fears, it felt logical at the time. I thought, *I'm their mom, it's my job to share my concerns. I don't want them blindsided, hurt, or taken advantage of.* But delivery is everything. What came across to my kids wasn't love or wisdom. It was a firehose of my fears.

Again, balance is the key. Yes, life has challenges, and it's our responsibility to prepare our children for them. Instead of overwhelming them with fear or painting a grim picture of the world, focus on building their resilience, resourcefulness, and courage. Show them how to face challenges head-on with adaptability and determination while also helping them marvel at the wonder of life. By striking this balance, we equip them to navigate life's complexities without losing sight of its magic.

Mastering your response + abilities means finding that balance: equipping your kids with the tools to grow, adapt, and navigate life's challenges with confidence, all while deepening the trust that anchors your relationship. That's the kind of leadership they'll remember and carry with them into the world.

Whew! That was a lot to take in. This chapter, *Mastering Your Response + Abilities,* was packed with powerful mindset shifts to help you build trust with your kids. Take your time. There's no rush. Revisit it as often as you need to fully absorb how each shifter can transform your family relationships and your life. Start with the one that resonates most and give it a try. Let's keep the momentum going as we slide into the next chapter, *Tools for Conversations, Connection,*

Mindset Shifts for Mastering Your Response + Abilities

and Understanding, which is loaded with strategies designed to deepen your understanding of and connection with your kids. Parents who weave these tools into the fabric of their family's culture experience greater joy, closeness, and mutual respect.

Chapter 6
Tools for Conversations, Connection, and Understanding

"There's no way to be a perfect mother and a million ways to be a good one."
~attributed to Jill Churchill

In this chapter, I'll share fun and effective tools to enhance your relationships with your kids. When you're present, engagement is felt, conversations flow, and quality time is shared. Guided by M8 #2, Begin with the End in Mind, these tools will help you become an influential and trusted leader. They're designed to strengthen your connections and make your relationships more enjoyable. Here are a handful of those million ways…

Know Your Superpowers

We all have something special that sets us apart: our unique superpowers, the innate gifts and talents that make us shine and bring something extraordinary to the world. Let's delve into what it means to recognize, celebrate, and balance these superpowers in ourselves and our families.

Everyone has a superpower—actually, more than a few. Think about one of yours for a moment. What natural gifts or talents come to mind? What qualities make you, well, you? These are what I call your superpowers: the strengths that set you apart and that the world needs. They're like your own special spices added to the soup pot of humanity, making it tastier, heartier, and better. But like anything else, even superpowers need balance. When they're out of balance, they get distorted, shifting from super awesome to super ineffective. And going back to the soup pot analogy, too much of your special spice could make the soup too salty, too spicy, or inedible. That makes sense, right? Balance is always a good thing.

Take one of my superpowers, for example; I'm a big-time giver. I love giving my time, effort, and resources to those in my world. It brings me tremendous joy to see the happiness it creates. But when I overextend myself, my giver superpower becomes ineffective, turning that joy into a very bad mood. I can feel the distortion taking shape: the resentment, exhaustion, and irritation from not being appreciated. My giving turns from a strength into a liability. Think about one of your superpowers and what happens when it crosses the line into Distortion-ville. Being aware of this is your first step toward balance.

One of my clients has the superpower of resilience. She's faced more than her fair share of challenges: debilitating health issues, the death of her spouse, raising kids on her own, and rebuilding her career from scratch. She's a true superhero. She has unstoppable kindness, reliability, optimism, and drive. Yet, even her resilience, when pushed to extremes, has its limits. Knowing she can handle more than most, she often takes on too much, pushing herself to the point of burnout. Ironically, it's this very resilience that leads her to over-commit and experience the inevitable crash and burn. The strain affects her already compromised health, leaving her extra fatigued, short-tempered, and irritable with her kids. Her greatest strength now becomes the source of her struggles.

The lesson here is all about balance. Your superpowers, those special traits that make you unique, are essential to bring forward in your life as long as they empower you, not stress you. The same goes for your children. Helping them recognize and honor their superpowers is not only a fun process, but it can also strengthen family bonds and create a deeper appreciation for one another.

So, what are the superpowers of your family members? Take some time to explore this together, whether over a meal, on a hike, or during a car ride. Pick a moment when everyone is relaxed and open to talking. Start by explaining the concept of superpowers and sharing yours to give them an example, and then ask your kids to share theirs. You might be pleasantly surprised by what they reveal. This conversation can be an enjoyable and insightful way to create more appreciation for one another.

But don't forget to talk about the flip side, about what happens when superpowers get distorted. Share examples from your own life to help your kids understand the importance of balance. By creating this awareness of their superpowers, you empower them to keep these strengths in balance, ensuring they remain assets rather than liabilities.

Here are some examples:

Superpower	**Distortion**
Giver	Exhausted, resentful
Tenacious	Burnout, don't know when to stop
Loyal	Lacks boundaries, enables others
Compassionate	Hyper-sensitive, worried

Reasons for Seasons, Your Child's Natural Rhythm

As parents, we all want to see our kids brimming with life, energy, and vitality, much like the beautiful blooms of spring that take our breath away. Spring is the season when everything seems to come alive and feels vibrant and fresh. And just as nature flourishes after a restful winter, so do our children. Think about it: winter, with its shorter days, chilly air, and nourishing rains, is nature's way of preparing the earth (and us) for the explosion of renewed energy. Without winter's rest, there's no springtime bloom.

Parents, Grow Up!

Think about winter for a sec. Are you a ball of energy ready to conquer the world? I doubt it. You're probably cocooned in a blanket, rocking those comfy sweatpants and fuzzy slippers, with a hot drink in hand, just soaking in this slower-paced season. Totally natural! When spring arrives, new energy surges, and you're ready to take on anything.

This ebb and flow of energy isn't just a seasonal quirk; it's part of life's rhythm, affecting us all. Each season plays a vital role, and tuning into these rhythms can make us better parents and more attuned leaders. Before you start wondering why your kids aren't focused, energetic, or motivated, ask yourself this: Are you planting corn in the fall and expecting a harvest in winter? It's a recipe for disappointment because every season has its purpose, and trying to rush nature is, well, impossible.

We all want our kids to be healthy and whole. We dream of them being self-competent and confident in building their lives. We want them to be curious and to tap into their full potential. We want them to have quality friends, volunteer, join clubs, play sports, play an instrument, be in a play, and plan for their future. But here's the thing: expecting them to be in a perpetual state of spring is unrealistic. None of us are wired to go full throttle all the time. Just like nature, we all have our unique rhythms and cycles.

Downtime isn't a luxury, and it's certainly not laziness. It's essential to our well-being. It's in those quieter, slower periods that we retreat, restore, and strengthen. We've become so focused on the go-go-go and do-do-do that we forget the importance of catching our breath, grounding ourselves, and refueling. Quality sleep and rest are an integral part of a healthy mind and body. They make the vitality of spring possible.

Take a moment to honestly assess your expectations. Where is your child right now in their seasonal cycle? Are they bursting with energy or in a phase of restoration? Understanding and respecting these natural rhythms can create more harmony and flow in your family. Support the beauty and necessity of your children's seasonal cycles.

Tools for Conversations, Connection, and Understanding

Listen, Hear, See, Feel

How are your listening skills? Listening is one of the most valuable and rewarding abilities we can develop as parents. When we truly listen, we gain incredible insight into our children's thoughts, feelings, and the unique world they live in. When you listen, you hear. You hear their tone. You hear what is not being said. When you listen, you see. You see their facial expressions and body language. When you listen, you feel. You feel the emotions behind their words. You feel their energy.

Real listening means being fully and completely present. It means being open to the entire experience of receiving. It's a sacred act of meeting them where they are and not where you are, where you think they should be, or thinking about your response should be and not hearing them. It requires our time, presence, and attention. When our kids feel this, we just might be lucky enough to receive their heart-speak and witness their vulnerability. That's special. That's sacred.

We all know at least one person who is an amazing listener in our lives. Ask yourself, why? By becoming a wonderful listener, you become a safe space, the motherlode of trust. In our fast-paced world, it's easy to get impatient and neglect the things that matter most in our relationships with our family: quality time, true presence, and sincere interest. When you really listen, you begin to understand your children. It's not easy being a good listener. Often, we're crafting our responses as we listen or feeling antsy because we want our turn to talk. Resist these urges and pull from M8 #6: Pain of Regret or Pain of Discipline and choose well. Hopefully, you'll choose to be disciplined in becoming an exceptional listener. Zip it, hold space, meet them where they are, and be grateful for the gift of receiving. You'll glean so much about what's going on in their world. What an honor.

As parents, even when we're not judgmental, our children often feel we are. Think of a time when you felt your mom or dad was judgmental, even though they would bet the farm they were caring and kind. How did it feel? These misinterpretations and misunderstandings don't just happen when we're young. They happen because the parent-child dynamic transcends age. I can give you a recent example with my mom. Anyone who knows me knows I'm not a fashionista. I consider myself a walking fashion faux pas. I'll choose comfort over style any day. I love my beat-up, baggy sweats, oversized t-shirts, unflattering yet super comfy bulky sweaters, and unmatched socks—my dog Lottie steals them. My mom often calls my attire "get-ups," and hey, she's right. I am the Get-up Queen! Happy, comfy, and content.

Recently, I was wearing one of my new bulky sweaters, which admittedly, isn't the most flattering. It makes me look boxy, like SpongeBob. But it's a favorite because it has a giant fuzzy smiley face on the front. I love it. It makes me happy. Every time I wear it, my students comment, "I love your sweater! It's so happy!" Which, of course, is why I love it. It makes people, including myself, happy.

When my mom saw it, I could tell she wasn't a fan. Not because she didn't think it was happy—she absolutely did—but because I looked like SpongeBob. And hey, that's fair. She had that disapproving expression that only her children could notice. You know what I'm talking about. It's the same disapproving expression I give my kids without even realizing it. So, when she saw me, she said, "Is that what you wore today?" Her tone was pleasant enough, but pleasant or not, we kids think we know exactly what that statement *really* meant. Even though I adore my mom, love her to pieces, respect her beyond words, and feel so lucky to be her daughter, I'm still the child (and remember, I'm sixty now), and she's the parent. Oh, the parent-child dynamics.

I initially felt irritated, then a twinge judged. This feeling lasted maybe twelve seconds before I snapped back to my calmer self and thought, *Here's what I know to be true: my mom is crazy about me and has been one of my biggest supporters throughout my life.* So, instead of feeling irritated and judged, I took her comment to mean *I love the smiley face, hate the fit!* You see my point.

Tools for Conversations, Connection, and Understanding

As parents, we are naturally attuned to our children's reactions, whether it's the tone of our voice, the way we deliver our words, or our facial expressions. It's part of the parenting journey to make comments, offer suggestions, and ask questions that challenge our children's perspectives and ideas. This is essential and applauded. But here's the magic sauce: It's all about delivery. If your goal is to strengthen your family's foundation and relationships, remain *curious*, be present, and expand the conversations with genuine interest

Ask thoughtful questions like, "What do you mean by that? Tell me more!" or "Can you walk me through your plan? I'm intrigued." or "I'd love to hear more about your idea. How did you come up with it?" These questions demonstrate your engagement and interest in learning about and understanding them.

Many parents I coach express concern that their kids barely talk to them. They often feel clueless about what's going on in their teen or young adult's world. The usual responses? A few head nods and the classic noncommittal one-syllable answers: "Yeah," "Nope," or the occasional "Meh." While this is typical during the teen years, normalizing it and missing opportunities to engage can cause the gap to widen as they move into adulthood.

If you want to bridge that gap and strengthen your connection, commit to becoming a legendary listener, the kind who masters the art of asking curious questions. This is where the magic happens. By being both fully present and genuinely curious, you create an engaging environment that fosters a reciprocal exchange of ideas. It's how you become one of their trusted peeps, wielding great influence. Earn their trust, and soon you'll have a seat at the table of their inner world.

Another essential part of listening is the art of observation. When we see our kids struggling with fears, heartbreak, insecurities, or anxieties, it's natural to want to take those on ourselves. But observing without absorbing is a powerful skill that allows us to truly support them. When we absorb their struggles, we unintentionally make it about us instead of them. Worse, we add to their burdens instead of helping lighten the load. Lose-lose, right? You see where I'm going with this.

Practicing this skill empowers both you and your children. Observing without absorbing lets you be the steady, supportive presence they need. Remember, preaching isn't teaching. Lead by example and meet them where they are. They don't need you to solve, fix, or repair anything. They need a safe place to exhale and be vulnerable. When you observe and listen, you show them you're present and are fully committed to being there. Hope you listened and heard me. Wink, wink...

Ask Your Children

How often do you ask your kids what they think about you? It might sound intimidating and a bit crazy, but asking for their honest feedback is a meaningful way to build trust. When you value their voices, opinions, and ideas, you show them that their perspective matters and that you genuinely care. This can be a challenging step for many parents, as it often stirs up reflections on the many layers of you we discussed in Chapter 1: your ego, beliefs, values, societal pressures, habits, and childhood experiences. Mustering the courage and vulnerability to ask, "How am I doing as your mom (or dad)?" can feel daunting, but it's an important step toward a healthy and respectful relationship.

To help you begin, here's a list of questions you can ask your children. The guidelines are simple: 1) only ask one or two questions to see how it goes, and 2) ask when it's just the two of you. This should be a private, intimate exchange. Never initiate this conversation in the presence of others; that can change the dynamics. People often act differently or feel influenced when others are around.

Choose a quiet time when it's just you and your child, when they seem open to a conversation. This could be during a walk, a drive, or when they're relaxed at home. Then, ask one (or two) of these questions:

Tools for Conversations, Connection, and Understanding

- What do you like/love about me?
- What do you not like about me?
- How could I improve?
- What do you need more/less of from me?
- How can I best support you?

Be sure to explain that there are no right or wrong answers. Emphasize that this is a judgment-free zone and that you truly value their feelings, thoughts, and your relationship. Approach the conversation without expectations. If you're initially met with resistance or a quick "We're good," don't be discouraged. Smile and gently let them know how much their feedback matters to you. Explain that their insights and feelings help you grow as both a person and a parent and that this will strengthen your relationship. Don't give up. Remind them how much you value your relationship and how precious it is to you.

When they do open up, you might be surprised or even delighted by what they share. Remember, this exercise is about understanding them and how they feel about you at this moment in their life. It's not about you, your feelings, or your pride. Your role is to listen without reacting and to value their voice. Apply the tools and lessons you've learned in this book. If your child says something you don't want to hear, like "You're super controlling," resist the urge to JED (Justify, Excuse, Defend), M8 #7. Avoid saying, "Well, I didn't want you to get bad grades," or "I was only trying to help because I didn't want to see you sad." Avoid the impulse to JED. Let them express their thoughts and feelings freely.

This exercise remains one of my favorites, even now, with my kids in their twenties. Regularly checking in with each other fosters closeness, strengthens our relationships, and cultivates healthy habits that will last a lifetime.

Table Talk for Champions

Are you starting to notice a pattern? Building trust takes time, presence, patience, and consistency. Over time, these efforts will create strong bonds. What truly matters is the *quality* of time spent together. For instance, you could be sharing a meal, but if you're distracted by your phone, checking texts or emails, that's not quality time—it's wasted time.

This brings us to the next treasured tool: Table Talk for Champions. This practice creates opportunities for you and your children to check in and share how things are going in your day-to-day lives. While gathering around the dinner table without distractions is wonderful, these conversations can also take place during a drive, on a hike, or even while lounging on the couch.

These conversations act as valuable checkpoints to reveal progress, setbacks, lessons, and goals. By making this a regular practice, you teach and empower your children to reflect on their choices, actions, and outcomes, promoting self-awareness and growth. Whether it's a daily, weekly, or even occasional ritual—whatever works best for your family—it's an intentional moment to connect. To guide the conversation, try asking:

- What was your biggest win today (or this week)?
- What was your biggest challenge?
- What lessons can you take from both your successes and setbacks?

Reflecting together allows everyone to feel part of each other's world while creating opportunities to learn, grow, and improve. When you encourage your children to identify lessons from their experiences, you help them develop the perspective and confidence to navigate life with greater adaptability and wisdom.

For parents whose kids might not open up or talk much, this is an invaluable tool. These questions are a gentle way to spark natural conversations. Don't expect a grand slam right away. Give them space to warm up. Stay consistent and show genuine interest in their week, just as you share yours with them. Make sure they feel that you're all in this together, playing on the same team. Table Talk for Champions is an excellent way to build camaraderie within your family tribe. Go, team, go!

Tools for Conversations, Connection, and Understanding

Blah, Blah, Blah, Ginger!

I'm a big fan of Gary Larson, the genius behind *The Far Side.* One of my all-time favorite cartoons, and one I've referenced countless times in both my personal and professional life, is Gary's 1983 "What We Say to Dogs," where a man is giving his dog, Ginger, a long list of instructions.[9] The first panel is captioned, "What we say to dogs," and the second, "What they hear": *Blah, blah, blah, Ginger! Blah, blah, blah, blah, blah, blah, Ginger! Blah, blah, blah...*

This cartoon perfectly captures what often happens when parents preach, instruct, or go full soapbox mode with their kids. Their eyes glaze over; they hear the noise but don't really listen. They might catch their name amidst the blah, blah, blahs, which snaps them out of their trance for about two seconds. We've all been there. We've all been both the blah-er and the blah-ee.

Now, if you're talking to hear your own voice, to feel important, in charge, or like the expert, then by all means, blah, blah away. But if your goal is actually to get your kids to listen (M8 #2, Begin with the End in Mind, *What's the goal? What outcome do you want?*), then you're missing the mark big time. There's a better way. Here's my question for you: Do you have the desire and discipline to get the results you are looking for? Yes, another Magnificent 8: #4, Desire and Discipline: The Dynamic Duo.

Your life experience is valuable; there's no question about that. But if you want your kids to hear you, really hear you, you need to make your wisdom relatable, relevant, and digestible. Instead of turning your message into a rant, approach them as both a leader and a teammate. Come to them, not at them. Engage with them in a way that helps you understand how they think, how to reach them, and ultimately, how to become someone they trust and want to listen to.

---

[9] "Blah, blah, blah, Ginger!" ("What We Say to Dogs" October 25, 1983 Gary Larson: https://www.thefarside.com/shop/comic-art-prints

Parents, Grow Up!

When you bombard them with a firehose of opinions, suggestions, or advice, you're not just wasting time; you're missing a golden opportunity to connect with them. And maybe even teach them something they'll carry with them forever.

You already know yourself pretty well. You know the way, because you've been there and done that and got the T-shirt. But now, it's their time. Their rite of passage is to be the rookies, the novices of life. Your job is to gently and deliberately guide them. You want to hear their plans, how they intend to solve problems, and why they want to take a certain path. This is about helping them learn to tackle their own challenges while equipping them with a toolkit full of options to succeed.

Empower them to become self-reliant by sharing these tools. Instead of saying, "You should do this..." or "You need to do that..." share your personal experiences of how these tools have helped you. Use what you've learned: pull from the M8, be a legendary listener, stay curious (not judgmental), ask thoughtful questions to get them to open up, and be present and engaged. You've got this!

So, how are you feeling? I hope you now have a deeper understanding of trust, its intricate and sometimes elusive layers, and the tools to nurture it within your family. Trust is the cornerstone of every healthy family, and Chapters 4, 5, and 6 have provided you with tools and strategies to strengthen this essential bond. Together, they've built the framework for respectful, enjoyable relationships to flourish.

Now, with layers of trust in place, it's time to add the next layer to your family dynamic: cultivating a culture of inspiration. In Chapter 7, you'll explore how to become one of your child's greatest influences, bringing both joyful motivation and meaningful inspiration into their lives.

Chapter 7
Be the Muse

"Leadership is not about being in charge. It is about taking care of those in your charge."
~Simon Sinek[10]

What happens when you feel inspired? How do you view those who inspire you?

For me, inspiration feels crazy good, like an avalanche of motivation barreling down a mountain, unstoppable, powerful, and exhilarating. It's that rush of adrenaline that drives me to action. When someone inspires me, I feel awe, respect, and admiration for their discipline, determination, and enduring dedication to their passions and goals. People with that kind of energy are magnetic. They inspire everyone around them. Honestly, I want to rub up against those inspiring people just to soak up their phenomenal energy!

No matter how you define it, inspiration is something we all want more of in our lives. It keeps us hopeful, motivated, and invigorated. And here's the best part: *You* can be that source of inspiration for your children. One of the most effective ways to encourage your kids

---

[10] Simon Sinek, *Leaders Eat Last: Why Some Teams Pull Together and Others Don't.* Portfolio, 2017.

to adopt healthy habits, master life's essentials, and pursue meaningful achievements is by inspiring them.

Let's be real. Wise words and knowledge are powerful, but actions are what ignite lasting inspiration. If you're going to use words of wisdom and share knowledge with your kids, make it count by pairing them with purpose-driven actions. As we've discussed, the culture you create at home becomes your children's normal. It's their training ground, their first glimpse of what family looks like, feels like, and acts like. Whether or not you take on this role deliberately, the responsibility of nurturing your children's well-being is yours. It's your job to love, protect, teach, prepare, and empower them. To do this effectively, you need to be an inspiring and influential leader; you need to be *the muse*.

So, how do you become the muse? How do you inspire your children to grow into confident, competent individuals? It starts with showing them the way and then guiding them through the process of mastering new skills and building confidence, one phase at a time.

Start with the four phases of learning:

1. Show them how—let them observe.
2. Do it together—talk them through it.
3. Watch them do it—let them talk you through it.
4. Let them do it independently.

These phases apply to everything you want your children to learn, from tying their shoes to writing thank-you notes, apologizing sincerely, cooking a favorite meal, and everything in between. They're the building blocks of mastery. But being the muse goes way beyond teaching skills; it's about modeling values and actions that inspire growth and progress. Being the muse means:

- Investing quality time with your children.
- Leading consistently with actions that reflect your values.
- Making an effort, even when you don't feel like it.
- Sticking to your commitments, no matter how challenging.
- Fortifying your family's ecosystem so it remains healthy and strong.

Be the Muse

By focusing on these principles, you empower your kids to become confident, self-reliant, and skilled in life's essentials. That's not only an act of love, but it's also an extraordinary way to inspire them to believe in themselves. And that belief? It's the root of all they'll accomplish. Every young person I coach who speaks highly of their parents points to what their parents *taught* them, not what they *bought* for them. One of my favorite examples comes from a teen who said, "I'm so glad my parents trusted me enough to take responsibility for my sports stuff. It feels good to handle my commitments—washing my uniform, packing my water bottles and snacks, and figuring out my rides to and from games. And it feels even better knowing my parents know I'm capable."

That's the power of being a muse. Your desire and discipline to teach, empower, and inspire your kids to be self-reliant and capable will be what they remember most and what they'll be most grateful for. Now *that's* inspiring.

The Muse's Toolbox

The four phases of learning give you the blueprint for being an inspiring leader to your children. Now, let's take it a step further. I'm about to share a robust collection of concepts and strategies designed to spark self-empowerment and build essential life skills for both you and your kids. These techniques are timeless, versatile, and impactful at any age. Seriously, this stuff gets me pumped up! I can't wait to share these tools with you and help you create an even stronger, more connected family. We'll begin with the 10 Wells of Wisdom.

The 10 Wells of Wisdom

I'm a sucker for a simple, no-nonsense list that helps me start and often reset my day. For years, I've shared the analogy of dipping into our inner wells of wisdom, which already contain everything we need. We often expend so much time and energy searching externally for answers or solutions when, in reality, they're already within us.

Parents, Grow Up!

My 10 Wells of Wisdom are at the heart of not just my parent empowerment program but also of a fulfilling life. When you integrate these 10 Wells into your family's mindsets and daily routines, you teach priceless lessons: how to care for yourselves, how to be whole, how to feel connected, and how to be truly well. As I often say, "To live well, you have to be well."

Welcome to the 10 Wells of Wisdom:

1. **Eat well.** Nourish and fuel yourself.
2. **Move well.** Elevate your mood, decrease stress, and strengthen your body.
3. **Sleep well.** Restore, rejuvenate, heal, and energize.
4. **Think well.** Your thoughts matter. Train your brain to work for you.
5. **Speak well.** Your words reflect who you are and resonate for a lifetime. Speak kindly.
6. **Choose well.** Your choices determine the direction and quality of your life.
7. **Give well.** Giving benefits both the giver and receiver, contributing to a caring world.
8. **Receive well.** You deserve it. Allow others the joy of giving.
9. **Play well.** Gather, giggle, grub, and gab with others.
10. **Dream well.** Dreams fuel imagination and inspiration. Let them illuminate your path forward.

Keep these Wells visible. Stick them on your fridge, your desk, or even your bathroom mirror. Let them become an inherent part of your parenting and family life. As with most things, start small. To begin with, focus on just one Well for yourself. When you experience a positive change, share your win. Lead by example instead of telling your children what to do.

Because they are interconnected, I recommend starting with the first three Wells, which I call "The Three Big Duhs." When you *eat well*, *move well*, and *sleep well*, you strengthen your mind and body, building a solid foundation for everything else. Um, duh!

Be the Muse

Once you've got the Three Big Duhs down, move on to Think Well. A calm and clear mind replaces anxiety and clutter. Then, Speaking Well leads to kinder conversations and healthier relationships. Giving Well and Receiving Well? They're like two peas in a pod. As the wise sentiment says, "It is in giving that we receive." Many of us find giving easier than receiving. I'm right there with you. It's something I'm still working on. I love giving, but I also remind myself that the joy I feel in giving is exactly what someone else wants to feel, too. Don't rob people of their joy by resisting their kindness. Accept it with a grateful heart.

The last two Wells often get pooh-poohed, but don't dismiss them! They are vital to your well-being. Playing Well connects you to others and enriches your life. Dreaming Well illuminates a purposeful path forward, filled with your heart's desires and your soul's calling.

These 10 Wells of Wisdom are well worth your time and commitment. Start or restart your day with them at any moment. That's their simplicity and brilliance. And speaking of restarts, let me introduce you to the next treasured tool I call Perpetual Arrival.

Perpetual Arrival

I vividly remember standing in the shower when I suddenly blurted out, "Perpetual Arrival!" The phrase perfectly captures what I emphasize with my students at every opportunity: "The quality of your future is determined by the quality of your now." Don't skim over that. This is a big, juicy, and delicious concept. Read it again: *The quality of your future is determined by the quality of your now*. Take this concept, and zoom in a bit closer to grasp.

Here's my idea of Perpetual Arrival: every single second brings a new moment, bursting with new opportunities that continually arrive—moment after moment. Each one is a chance to create or break a habit, to choose better thoughts, to feel differently, or to start again. Isn't this an incredible realization? I absolutely love the idea that we're perpetually greeting a new opportunity at every moment. When this epiphany soaked in, this realization was a WOW for me!

When we nurture the seed of *perpetual arrival* within our children, it awakens them to a whole new way of thinking and living. It makes them aware of the power they hold in every moment: the power to choose.

Perpetual Arrival confirms that we're in control of how we choose to live "that moment." Do we fuel fear? Anxiety? Negativity? Or do we use this moment to make things better? This mindset empowers us and our kids to make immediate course corrections instead of getting stuck in a spiral of regret. It lets them say, "You know what? I've got this. I've got a new moment and a fresh opportunity just around the corner."

The concept of perpetual arrival is one of the most transformative mindsets we can share with our kids. It keeps them aware, accountable, and empowered to shape their lives moment by moment. I'm absolutely obsessed with this mind-blowing idea, and I hope it inspires you as much as it has me.

Next are some of the easiest and greatest power tools you and your kids could ever use. No batteries needed, no charging required. These tools never lose their power. They're perfect for making wiser decisions and communicating with clear intention and kindness.

The Fantastic 5, Power Tools to Inspire

These next tools are absolute favorites among my students. They generate clarity, boost productivity, and light up new possibilities in any situation. Quick, effective, and easy to use, they fuel your kids' confidence and competence while delivering immediate results. Who doesn't want to feel confident in taking care of themselves? To be resourceful and self-reliant? Seriously, isn't that a universal desire? This is yet another opportunity to lead by example and inspire your kids to grab the baton and run with it!

By teaching your children how to use these tools, you're planting seeds of inspiration that can grow within them for a lifetime. Never underestimate the potency of these seemingly simple tools. Simple doesn't mean insignificant. Simple often means overlooked and underutilized. Time and time again, I find that the most joyful people build their lives with a steadfast commitment to mastering the basics.

Pros and Cons Power Tool

Almost everyone I've worked with says, "Of course, I know what pros and cons are!" But they also admit they rarely, if ever, put them into practice. It's typical. We know about these tools, but seldom do we use them. That's why I have great disdain for the saying, "When we know better, we do better." Ha! What a joke. Even when we know better, we don't do better. I know I resemble that statement more than I'd like to admit. Here's a great solution...

A pros-and-cons list is so simple, so basic, and that's exactly what makes it brilliant. I'm all about the basics, and a pros-and-cons list is like a good bra, a good sunscreen, and a good friend: it offers strong support, reliable protection, and always comes through when you need it most.

Before introducing this tool to your kids, show them how you use it in your own life. For example, create a pros-and-cons list for a decision you're facing and let them see its impact firsthand. Better yet, invite them to contribute by adding a few pros and cons to your list. Together, you'll experience the clarity that emerges and the relief of discovering a wiser path forward.

Now it's their turn. Have them apply the same process to something in their world. Should they go to a party with one friend or spend the day at a museum with another? Should they save for concert tickets or splurge on sneakers? Should they email their teacher to express a concern or ignore it? Walk them through it without projecting your opinions or fears. The goal is to guide, not manage.

Whenever your kids face a decision, whether it's big or small, easy or tough, encourage them to make a pros-and-cons list. They might be surprised by the outcome or find that their gut feeling was spot on. Either way, it's a fast and effective method for making smarter choices or for taking a calculated risk while fully understanding the potential downsides. It's a life skill everyone should master. Don't make an important decision without it!

Do-Over Power Tool

Wow, do I love do-overs! I use this tool almost daily, and many parents I coach say it's one of their go-to strategies for improving relationships with their kids. The magic of do-overs shines brightest when a parent initiates it for their children. It breaks down the illusion that parents are perfect or have all the answers, showing vulnerability in a way that develops a special kind of closeness. After all, no one likes a know-it-all or someone who acts like they can do no wrong.

When parents are willing to admit their mistakes in front of their kids, trust and inspiration grow. For example, stopping mid-sentence to say, 'I didn't say that well. Can I have a do-over to try again?' shows your commitment to learning and improving while also demonstrating the respect and importance you place on your relationship with your children.

The real power of a do-over lies in leading by example, by showing your kids that making mistakes is part of being human, as long as you hold yourself accountable and make things right. Owning up to your blunders reveals the strength of your character, humility, and great leadership—qualities that will inspire your family.

Permission Power Tool

The word "permission" often makes people cringe or even rebel. It can feel like a restriction on freedom, making us uneasy or even inferior. And sure, those feelings might be valid in some contexts, but that's not where we're headed here.

Starting today, I want you to see "permission" in a whole new light. See it as one of your communication superpowers with your kids. As always, you're leading by example, teaching your children to become masterful communicators by putting this tool into practice.

The permission power tool is closely tied to the art of being a legendary listener. When you're listening and feel the itch to offer your opinion, that's your cue to pause and reach for this tool. Instead of cannonballing in with your thoughts, ask your child if they're open to hearing them. Yes, you ask for permission. Resist the urge to unload and instead, pull from any of the M8s to support you. This is the time to ask if they're looking for support, whether it's validation, commiseration, or help brainstorm solutions.

This approach works wonders. It might look something like this: when you want to share something and hope they'll be open to it, ease in gently. You could say, "I can see you're really emotional (or mad, or upset) right now. Would you be open to hearing a different perspective?" This is far more effective than bulldozing through their emotions with something like, "It's hard for me to believe you don't see the obvious," which is almost guaranteed to make them shut down or explode.

When you gently ask, whether it's, "Would you be willing...," "Are you open to...," or "May I offer...," nine times out of ten, your child will naturally soften and be more willing to listen. Even better, they'll be more likely to share their feelings with you next time. This strengthens your relationship and makes them more likely to reciprocate.

We've all felt that moment when someone we love comes at us full force with their opinions and beliefs. We shut down and hear nothing. Delivery is everything. Masterful communicators understand the power of thoughtful delivery. At any age, it's a skill that fosters both respect and reverence.

Nonnegotiables Power Tool

When I talk about nonnegotiables, I'm referring to dealbreakers or walk-aways. These are the inner boundaries that protect your values and uphold your self-worth. Without them, you're not just inviting chaos into your life, you're creating it. I see nonnegotiables as a mix of self-worth, values, and beliefs. They act as gatekeepers, honoring what truly matters most and setting healthy limits. Once you commit to them, your nonnegotiables become well-defined and nonnegotiable (pun intended).

Parents, Grow Up!

In all my years of teaching and coaching self-empowerment, I've rarely met anyone, regardless of age, who has intentionally taken the time to define their nonnegotiables. Most people think they can rattle them off, but when asked, I usually get a long pause, followed by, "Hmmmmm...good question! I need to think about this."

Nonnegotiables aren't whimsical or fleeting. They uphold your moral code and character, serving as your personal compass. When I picture my nonnegotiables, I think of an impenetrable lighthouse—solid, sturdy, purposeful, and unwavering. The lighthouse is there to guide me back to safety when I'm lost or to light the way forward when the path is unclear. Either way, it stands firm as a reminder of what keeps me aligned with my values.

Nonnegotiables are unique to each person. We all have different stories, lessons, and journeys. Having clear nonnegotiables helps you stay true to yourself and your values. They are especially crucial when starting a relationship. Without them, you risk getting blindsided, walked over, or caught in the wrong current. Like a lighthouse, your nonnegotiables will light your path, keeping you on course.

The purpose of nonnegotiables is that they force you to get real about what matters most to you: your relationships, your career, and everything else that shapes your world. Take one of mine, for example. Since I was twenty, dating a cigarette smoker has been a hard no. Nope. Nada. The smell, the ashes, the whole vibe...just no. Dating a smoker would be like throwing a lit match at one of my core values: taking care of my health. There was never a gray area. Another dealbreaker? A job with a long, soul-sucking commute. After a quick pro-con list (pro: none; con: everything), I confirmed that spending hours in traffic was not my idea of living the dream. Hard pass.

Now, had I ignored these nonnegotiables—dated Mr. Marlboro Man or taken that grueling commute—you'd be meeting a different Jill. We're talking Mean Jill. Overheated Jill. Edgy, Ma-a-a-d Jill. Why? Because I would've stomped all over my values, disrespected my self-worth, and would be wallowing in regret.

Be the Muse

This all ties perfectly into one of the M8s, the Pain of Regret or the Pain of Discipline. Spoiler alert: discipline wins every time. The takeaway: Stick to your nonnegotiables. They're not just rules; they're lifelines to a happier, healthier you.

Teaching your kids to identify their nonnegotiables will help them construct their inner lighthouses. And if you haven't built yours yet, now's the perfect time. This is such a meaningful and enlightening conversation to have with your kids, one that just might stay with them for a lifetime.

F.O.O.T. Power Tool

Few things derail productivity faster than a frazzled brain juggling too many tasks. Hauling around an unrealistic to-do list? That's a one-way ticket to sabotaging your progress *and* your peace of mind. Enter the F.O.O.T. power tool: focus on one thing. I get it. This idea might sound impossible when you're facing a mountain of priorities, but that's exactly why F.O.O.T. will help. It's a reminder to pause, take a hard look at your to-do list, and re-examine those priorities.

Let a few things slide for now, at least. It's better to do one thing exceptionally well—I mean really knock it out of the park—than to do many things subpar.

When our minds are overloaded with endless to-dos, overwhelm paralyzes productivity, clouds clarity, and piles on unnecessary stress. That's where F.O.O.T. comes in to save the day. By focusing on one thing, this tool quiets the mental noise, anchors you in the present, and gives you the clarity needed to carve out a path for real progress. So lace up and put your best F.O.O.T. forward—and empower your family to do the same.

The Fantastic 5 Power Tools are timeless gems—practical strategies your family might end up using every single day. Teaching these techniques to your kids and practicing them together strengthens their competence and confidence in making wiser decisions as they navigate their lives. By guiding them, you're leading by example and helping them create a life they love. Bravo!

Say it Now, Celebrate Now!

Every time I attend a life celebration, I'm overcome with a mix of emotions: awe at a life well-lived intertwined with the grief of finality. Remembering someone is always bittersweet—deep gratitude for the memories they left behind, mingled with the heartache of knowing the chance to express what we feel and to say the words we wish we had, is forever gone. The finality hits hard, lodging a lump in the throat as the weight of what's left unsaid settles in, heavy and undeniable.

Have you ever felt this way? That gnawing thought of "I wish I'd said..." echoing long after it's too late? These moments are jarring reminders of how precious time is and how much we take for granted the chance to share our feelings while we still can.

With this awareness in mind, I passionately encourage every parent, every person, to start a new family tradition: celebrating and honoring your loved ones while you're still here together. Make birthdays more than just cake and candles. Use them as an opportunity to speak from the heart, to share your love, admiration, and favorite stories. Imagine the impact of saying, out loud, what you see in them, why they matter, and the ways they've made your life better. Say it Now, say it proud while you can.

The pain of regret is one of life's heaviest burdens (again, a perfect opportunity to fire up M8 #6: Pain or Regret of Pain of Discipline). Instead of carrying this weight, you can choose discipline. You can choose to make this birthday celebration, Say it Now, a new family tradition. Your words are like seeds planted deep in their hearts, where they'll grow, fed by the understanding that they're truly seen, valued, and loved by the people who matter most.

There's a saying by James Clear: "Feel compliments as deeply as you feel insults."[11] Let your belief in your family members be known, felt, and celebrated. These are the words they might cling to in their darkest moments or the light that guides them through. Those words are a true gift; they become their inner voice. Make them memorable long after the birthday presents have been forgotten.

Let this inspire you to say it now. Celebrate now. There's no better time to start than whoever's birthday is next!

Sharing our love and gratitude at the moment strengthens bonds and creates lasting memories. But life isn't always clear or easy, and thankfully, there's a wealth of wisdom passed down through the ages from those who've walked this path before us. Their insights serve as guiding lights when we need them most. Let's take a look at one of these timeless sage tools...

Sage Giants

Imagine this: We're all hiking up the mountain of life, and while the view might be breathtaking, the trail can get a bit rocky. But here's the good news: We're not the first ones to trek this path. In fact, we're standing on the shoulders of sage giants who've already blazed the trail. These wise souls—whether they're philosophers like Socrates, your third-grade teacher, your barber, your grandparents, or even Winnie the Pooh—have shared their wisdom to help us navigate the tricky terrain of self-love, self-worth, and our life's purpose.

Isn't that great news? We are not alone and don't need to reinvent the wheel. Instead, let's focus on putting our best F.O.O.T. forward—that's focus on one thing—and reach for the tools these giants have bestowed upon us. They've lit up the path with insights to bring more ease, joy, and peace into our lives. And the best part? By embracing their wisdom, we keep it alive and empower others as we pass it on.

Take Don Miguel Ruiz's *Four Agreements*, for example. Thanks, Don! This simple yet powerful tool is like a Swiss Army knife for

---

[11] https://jamesclear.com/3-2-1/september-24-2020

personal growth: compact, versatile, and incredibly effective. Here's the cheat sheet:

1. **Be impeccable with your word**. Speak with integrity, kindness, and truth because your words have the power to create or destroy.
2. **Don't take things personally.** What others say or do is a reflection of them, not you, so don't carry burdens that aren't yours to bear.
3. **Don't make assumptions.** Replace guesswork with curiosity; ask questions and seek clarity instead of jumping to conclusions.
4. **Always do your best**. Give your all in any situation, not for perfection, but for the peace of knowing you've tried your best.

These agreements aren't just valuable for us grown-ups; they're also an excellent tool for parents to teach their kids as they begin to navigate their own trails. If you're in the mood to dive into the whole book, by all means, go for it! But even if you and your family just start with these four gems today, you're already ahead of the game.

And who knows? These principles might inspire you to craft your own family agreements, ones that resonate with your tribe. Remember, the wisdom of those who came before us—and those still with us—is like an open treasure chest, brimming with timeless gems of enlightenment. We don't lack the tools or knowledge; we just need to put them to use. So, embrace these treasures, and when the time comes, share them with your children, the next generation of sage trailblazers.

The wisdom of Sage Giants reminds us that we have everything we need to guide us through life's adventures if we're willing to listen and learn. But while we draw strength and insight from those who came before us, life also requires us to trust in the unknown, to release our grip on control, and to embrace the art of letting go, especially with our children.

Hold On Loosely (And yes, that awesome song by 38 Special definitely comes to mind.)

We've all learned the hard way what happens when we cling too tightly. It often backfires, giving us the exact opposite of what we hoped for. As parents, this might be one of the toughest challenges: learning to hold on loosely to our children. Our instincts scream at us to protect them from pain, to guide them down what we think is the best path. But one of our greatest responsibilities is to prepare them to fly, not on our backs or in our slipstream, but with their own wings. It's about trusting ourselves and, even more importantly, trusting them.

From the moment they entered our lives, we've been preparing for this gradual letting go. You'll always have a hold on their hearts, just as they will on yours. We brought them into this world to love, accept, and respect them for who they are, to celebrate their unique gifts, and to support them as they explore life's journey. They'll continue to grow, morph, and evolve, just as you did and still do.

Be their muse as they learn to ride the waves of their newfound interests. Encourage them to breathe life into fresh ideas and see where they lead. Teach them not to fixate on outcomes but to leave space for possibilities. If they dream of becoming a veterinarian in third grade, let them. If they want to rock out as a drummer in fifth grade, let them. And if, by high school, they're cooking up a storm and aiming to be a chef, let them. Childhood is when imagination should run free. These dreams may only last a season, but short-lived pursuits are still very valuable. Trying to confine them to a lane that fits your desires, fears, or expectations doesn't just stifle their happiness, wellness, and wholeness. It can also strain, even damage, your relationship with them.

Hold on loosely during these times of transition. Embrace the ever-evolving person they are becoming. Encourage them to try as many things as possible to discover what excites them, what ignites them, and what leaves them cold. Passion, or even simple curiosity, is a beautiful thing, and it's exactly what you want for them. And if their interests fizzle, don't panic. These moments of trial and error are how they learn about themselves, not just about what you want for them. Their purpose is theirs alone. Help them tune into their hearts, minds, and intuition. They are creating their story, their journey. Let them write, tell, and live it their way.

When we honor their journey, they learn to honor themselves much earlier. But when we impose our journey on them, we stifle their truths, talents, and momentum. There's a reason and a season for everything. Resist the urge to push them into a future-proof career path. (Nothing is "future-proof" without Desire and Discipline. Thanks, M8 #4.) More often than not, it backfires, robbing them of the chance to pour their heart and soul into something they truly love. Don't let fear or pride create a divide.

It's your responsibility, and their right, to have the space to discover what lights them up. Let them know how vital it is to listen to their hearts. Inspiring your children to take responsibility for the quality of their lives is the ultimate goal. It's a truth they'll carry forever, shaping every aspect of their future. Remember the ten most powerful two-letter words: If It is to Be, It is Up to Me, M8 #3.

Another quote I love to share with students and parents, often attributed to Howard Thurman, is: "Don't ask yourself what the world needs. Ask yourself what makes you come alive and go do that, because what the world needs are people who have come alive." This sentiment is one of the best conversation-starters and heart-openers you'll ever find.

Ask your children what makes their hearts come alive. If the word "alive" trips them up, offer words like "intrigues" or "piques your interest." Whether they're ten or thirty, age doesn't matter; this conversation is always relevant. Dive into what lights them up and sparks their curiosity. And don't forget to share what makes you come alive, too. Showing them that evolution is a lifelong journey gives them permission to explore more than one interest. Start the conversation and be open to boundless possibilities!

Be the Muse

Hopefully, the above tools have you pumped up to step into your role as the muse for your family to inspire them to reach their greatest heights. To be inspired by someone is to feel awe for their efforts and actions. It's that spark of motivation that ignites progress, the respect and gratitude that make you want to follow in their footsteps. As parents, leading by example is the ultimate form of inspiration. It shows your kids that the tools you teach are the same tools you live by.

Your commitment to your growth and your continuing to grow, improve, and evolve will light the way for your kids. They'll be inspired by how you show up, stick to your values, and take action.

To keep the inspiration flowing, I'm excited to share some family activities designed to strengthen your bond and spark plenty of laughter. These activities will add more giggles, meaningful conversations, creative ideas, and shared memories to your family's unique story. It's where inspiration meets action, bringing fun and unforgettable experiences to your everyday lives.

Chapter 8
The Muse Method: Family Activities That Bond and Brighten

"If your actions inspire others to dream more, learn more, do more, and become more, then you are an excellent parent."
~Attributed to John Quincy Adams

Welcome to a chapter filled with inspiration in action! This is where your role as the muse comes to life in a dynamic and hands-on way. Whether it's diving into meaningful conversations, sharing favorite quotes that spark curiosity and epiphany, or creating something special as a family, these moments enliven and celebrate your connection. You'll laugh together over shared stories, dream up adventures, and discover new traditions that bring fun and togetherness to your everyday lives.

Let the inspiration begin with these playful and purposeful activities.

Conversation Jar

I'm known as the "Quote Queen" by those who know me well. Quotes are my thing. They're not just conversation starters; they're tiny powerhouses of wisdom, humor, and inspiration waiting to be unleashed. When you let them (letting is the key), they can shift your perspective, spark motivation, stir your soul, or simply make you laugh. Quotes can come from anywhere and anyone—philosophers, historians, family, friends, celebrities, teachers, movies, bumper stickers, or even your own clever quips.

Okay, let's bring on the fun! Grab a jar, box, or container that catches your eye and make it your family's official Conversation Jar. Share the idea with your crew and invite everyone to contribute their favorite quotes whenever inspiration strikes. To get things rolling, ask everyone to find five quotes they enjoy and toss them in right away. Instant conversation fuel!

Then, when you're together at meals, on road trips, or during a lazy day at home, pull a quote from the jar, read it aloud, and let the conversation flow. What does it mean to each person? What's the reason behind why this person chose this quote? How might this apply to your lives? You'll quickly discover that interpretation is delightfully and sometimes annoyingly subjective. You'll uncover shared perspectives, surprising differences, and maybe even a few aha moments.

The best part? You'll get a peek into your kids' minds, their unique outlook on the world, and, more importantly, their world. A single quote might kindle curiosity or awaken new possibilities they hadn't considered before. Some quotes may even stick with your family and guide you through the years.

So, choose your quotes thoughtfully, share them openly, and let the magic of words bring your family closer, one conversation at a time.

And as your Conversation Jar stimulates these insightful discussions, imagine building on that energy. What if those words become actions, a way of living as a family? That's where the next Muse Method comes in, reminding us just how impactful words can be.

Words of the Week

As I've said time and time again, words hold immense power. That old saying, "Sticks and stones may break my bones, but words will never harm me," is an absolute eye-roller and, quite frankly, a load of dung in my fiery (and accurate) opinion. Do I really need to explain why this is preposterous? If words were truly harmless, mental, emotional, and verbal abuse wouldn't exist. We wouldn't have a trillion-dollar industry built around therapy, counseling, coaching, and mentoring dedicated to healing, empowering, and rebuilding lives. Words are like energetic beings, settling in our minds and taking up residency in our bodies, shaping how we move through the world.

Words *do* matter. They can create magic or mayhem. They can propel us forward or set us back, drive us closer, or drive us apart. The way we use words shapes our self-image, our relationships, and the ecosystem of our home. As a parent, you have an incredible opportunity to model the kind of words that encourage and inspire. Let words work their magic to bring your family closer.

A creative and fun way to create closeness is to gather your crew and choose a word or phrase to focus on for the week and infuse intention into those words. It could be a new vocabulary word, a mantra, or a theme that everyone agrees on. Brainstorm together and pick something that resonates; it's more likely to stick when everyone feels part of the process.

For instance, if your family chooses "Get it done!" as the phrase of the week, weave it into everything, whether it's tackling homework, completing chores, walking the dog, or simply maintaining a positive, can-do attitude. Or, pick a word that represents a specific focus for the week, like "adapt," "pause," or "lighten up." Let it serve as a guide, helping everyone stay centered and intentional about embracing that sentiment. At the end of the week, come together and share how it influenced or supported you.

Or get creative. Make a family shoutout like the ones athletes do before a big game to pump everyone up: "Never quit!" or "Gooooo

Parents, Grow Up!

Team!" I've seen families take it a step further by creating family swag: t-shirts, hats, mugs, magnets, or even a family plaque prominently mounted in their family room with their family's favorite phrase. Another fun idea is to create a Word Wall, where you display each week's phrase as a visual reminder for everyone. Better yet, insist that everyone has to use it with the family that week.

The possibilities are endless, and their impact is lasting. This activity isn't just about expanding vocabulary or focusing thoughts; it's about teaching your kids how words can shift moods, reshape thinking, and influence how they view themselves and the world around them. Plus, it builds a strong team spirit one word at a time.

As your family builds a camaraderie over intentional words and phrases, why not carry that connection to the table? Meals nourish more than just our bodies. They bring everyone together in a way that feels natural. And when everyone pitches in to prepare the meal, the magic multiplies. Good eats, great laughs, and cherished memories? Yes, please!

Meals Keep It Real

Sharing food is the ultimate love language. It's a universal way to connect. There's something quite special about gathering around the table, sharing stories, and savoring a meal as a family. Eating together? That's great. But cooking together? Now we're talking! It's a fantastic way to spend quality time, share a ton of laughs, and maybe even discover a hidden chef in the family.

The key here? Keep it simple and fun. This isn't about creating a Michelin-star meal or mastering complicated recipes. Stress and frustration? Not on the menu. In fact, the messier and sillier, the better!

Grab your squad and get started. The secret sauce? Pull from M8 #2, Begin with the End in Mind. Ask yourself, "What's the goal here?" If it's fun, laughter, and a delicious meal, you're already winning. Go with the flow, keep it easy, and don't overthink it—think personal pizzas, taco salads, nachos, or build-your-own-sandwich, burrito, or sundae bar. The objective? Good times, good grub, and good memories. And don't forget the tunes! Crank up the disco classics, pop hits, or a playlist the kids create. Music has a way of bringing everyone together. Who says dinner prep can't double as a dance party? Let go of the pressure to make everything post-worthy and focus on the real joy of togetherness. Who knows, you might just create a new family favorite—or at least a story to tell for years to come. ("Remember when Dad set the taco shells on fire?" Classic!)

After sharing laughs and good eats, let's keep that creative momentum going! It's time to bring your family's unique energy to life, literally, by designing something that celebrates who you are as a team.

Family Design

This activity is a favorite among the families I coach, and it's easy to see why. Whether you've got budding Picassos or self-proclaimed stick-figure champions, this project is a fun way to recognize your one-of-a-kind clan. It's not about who's the best artist; it's about coming together, sharing ideas, and creating something that represents the heart of your family. Gather everyone for a brainstorming session, where no idea is too wild or too wacky. Every contribution matters, and celebrating those individualistic ideas is half the fun. The process itself is just as meaningful as the final product. It's a chance to honor each voice and make sure everyone feels included. Once the ideas are flowing, refine them as a team, and then dive into designing your masterpiece: an emblem that truly reflects your family.

You might include the first letter of each family member's name, a number that holds significance, or even a beloved pet as your family mascot. The result? A one-of-a-kind family crest or logo that you can proudly plaster on t-shirts, hats, jackets, flags, or stationery. Feeling bold? Some families have even turned their design into a tattoo, a permanent badge of family pride!

To keep the creative juices flowing, set the mood with some good tunes to create good vibes. Choose a playlist that lifts everyone's spirits, whether it's upbeat dance tracks or nostalgic favorites.

Parents, Grow Up!

Encourage each person to add their personal flair through the design, colors, textures, fonts, or how the final piece should be showcased. The key here is to accept everyone's input and let go of perfectionism. Enjoy the process. Stay loose and flexible. And who knows? This project might reveal hidden artistic talents or inspire new family traditions. No matter what the finished piece looks like, the time spent creating together will be a memory you'll all cherish.

Now that you've tapped into your family's creativity and shared some laughs along the way, it's time to shift gears and dream big. What do you want to do together next week, next month, or even next year? That's where the Let's-Do-It list comes in.

Let's-Do-It List

Forget the bucket list. Who wants to wait for someday? It's time to take on a more proactive and exciting approach. It's time for the Let's-Do-It list! This isn't about later; this is about now. Get ready for serious fun as you dream big, and let your imagination run wild. It's a chance to explore wishes, simple pleasures, and bold desires together as a family.

Everyone gets a say in the Let 's-Do-It list. No idea is off limits, whether it's "let's hike every mountain in North America" or "let's make the last Tuesday of every month Taco Tuesday." The key? Keep it judgment-free, no eye-rolling, no scoffing, or no dismissing anyone's ideas. This list is a ceremony of possibility; welcome it all.

Once your list is ready, grab a calendar and start mapping out when and how you'll make each activity happen. Don't just talk about it; actually do it! There's no rush to cram everything into one month. Instead, gather as a family, set a realistic timeline, and use a year-long calendar to see the big picture. Planning it out makes it feel real. Counting down to those marked dates turns anticipation into one of the most exciting parts of the whole experience!

And let's be honest, some ideas might not be your thing, and that's okay. Roll with it anyway, and find your role in making the experience special. When my daughter suggested skydiving, my gut reaction was, "Hard pass." But I was outvoted. So, instead of nixing

The Muse Method: Family Activities That Bond & Brighten

her idea, I found my roles: I became the driver, snack provider, the pre-jump cheerleader, and memory capturer. I didn't jump, but being part of their adventure turned it into one of my most thrilling memories.

These shared experiences will bring richness to your family's story. They'll boost your camaraderie, strengthen your connection, and fill your lives with joy. Lead the way in making it happen.

The Let's-Do-It list is all about experiencing things as a family and creating wonderful and unforgettable memories. But sometimes, it's the simple words we say, like "I love you," that leave the most lasting impression. Words, just like experiences, can stay with us forever, especially when we take the time to show what they truly mean.

When I Say "I Love You"

Selena, one of my students and one of the wisest souls I've met, shared a beautiful exercise during one of our sessions. She'd been reading *Loveability* by Dr. Robert Holden, Ph.D., a book that explores how we can deepen our connections by reflecting on what we truly mean when we say, "I love you." Dr. Holden explains that those three little words can lose their meaning and impact if we don't take the time to understand what they represent for ourselves and for the person hearing them.

So, Selena and I decided to give it a try. We took a thoughtful moment to reflect on the meaning behind those words. Then, with heartfelt sincerity, she looked at me and said, "When I say I love you, this is what I mean…"

She shared things about me I didn't even realize she noticed, things that made me pause, smile, and think, "Wow, she really sees me." She told me how inspiring I was to her, and I couldn't help it; my eyes welled up with happy tears. That moment was unforgettable, a gift I'll treasure forever. Now, when Selena says, "I love you," she adds, "And you know what I mean." And oh, do I! It was one of those *wow* moments that makes your heart feel like it's tripling in size, infused with pure happiness.

Parents, Grow Up!

Since then, I've woven this practice into my life, not just with my family but with friends, too. Now, when I say, "I love you, and you know what I mean..." it's met with smiles, giggles, sometimes happy tears, and hearts that feel fuller. It's such an uplifting exchange.

Again, words matter. They're magic spells that bring us closer together. From now on, let's make sure phrases like "I love you," "I respect you," "I believe in you," "I trust you," or "I'm proud of you" speak to the heart and clearly express what we really mean. Too often, these meaningful phrases can feel meaningless. But with this simple practice, you can make your kids feel truly seen. It's a beautiful two-way street. When you say, "I love you" (or "respect you," "trust you," or "believe in you"), you'll know exactly what it means, and more importantly, so will they.

Our kids already know we love them, but what they really crave is to be understood, seen, and heard. Isn't that what we all want? Imagine how it would have felt if our parents had done this for us. Taking the time to share what these loving phrases really mean creates a heart-to-heart connection with your kids that will never fade.

Here's an example of how to make it more personal: "I love how your nose is always cold on hot summer days. I love how you need your feet free from the covers because, otherwise, you'll totally freak out. I love your quirky pickle routine, how you'd rather sip pickle juice from the lid than from the jar." These statements don't just say "I love you," they shout, "I see you! I get you!" They tell your children you adore what makes them uniquely them.

So the next time you say "I love you," those words will carry all the little quirks and traits that make them who they are, and they'll know just how deeply you cherish them. I can't profess enough how powerful this is. It's about celebrating life and treasuring the moments you'll one day wish you'd expressed before the chance was gone.

But love isn't just spoken; it's shown. It's about how we show up for our kids, invest our time, and create meaningful moments they'll carry long after they've left the nest. That's the heart of the Just-Us tradition, which is a way to turn love into lasting memories, one adventure at a time.

Just-Us Tradition

One of the sweetest, most cherished lessons my mom passed down to me was creating a special, one-on-one tradition with each of my kids. It quickly became one of our family's most meaningful customs. These intentional moments of focused time with just one child at a time became some of our best memories. Even now, with my kids grown and independent (don't blink!), they'll tell you that those one-on-one adventures with either their dad or me were among their most treasured childhood experiences.

And talk about my kids hitting the family jackpot! My mom, the original champion of this tradition and who has always led by example, took my kids on their own adventures, enriching their lives and adding to the tapestry of their stories. To this day, she keeps the Just-Us tradition alive and strong with my kids. Priceless.

Let me triple-enthusiastically encourage you (and other trusted family members) to start your own Just-Us tradition. It's hands down one of the most heartwarming and downright magical things you can do. And here's a little reminder: These moments don't have to be extravagant, fancy, or complicated. It's not about the dollar signs; it's about the thoughtfulness, the quality of time, and the memories you create.

You could grab a sandwich and head to the park or dangle your feet off a pier while enjoying a warm cup of clam chowder. (That was my mom and my son's thing. They were always on a quest for the best clam chowder during their getaways!) Or how about walking barefoot on the beach, collecting shells, building sandcastles, and watching the waves roll in? It's often the simplest moments that stick with us the longest.

The real magic lies in discovering what lights up your kids. What are their interests? Their curiosities? Start there. By showing interest in what they love, you're sending a loud and clear message: *I see you. I care about who you are.* And next time? Flip the script.

Invite them into your world. Share your passions and interests, or try something entirely new together. There's something extra special about experiencing a first with someone you love; those shared discoveries are unforgettable.

Ultimately, the goal is to leave a lasting imprint on your children's hearts, one that reflects your love and inspires them. The more you invest in one-on-one time, the stronger your relationships will become.

Every moment of quality time together fills that feel-good bucket. So here's your opportunity: Make them feel treasured in a way they'll never forget. Those feelings will stay with them forever.

While spending one-on-one time with your kids creates unforgettable memories and strengthens your relationship, it's often the simple, everyday moments—like flipping through old photo albums or scrolling through digital images and videos—that bring just as much joy. Nostalgia and laughter remind us of where we've been and how far we've come.

The next Muse Method captures that magic with plenty of heartfelt moments.

Smiles, Giggles, and Awwws

Without fail, whenever my kids stumble upon my baby pictures, or really, any photos from my youth, their faces soften with that sweet mix of tenderness and bouts of snorts and cackles. And let's call it like it is: They're laughing at me, not with me. Rightfully so!

So, here's what you do: Pull out your baby pictures and share them with your kids. It's pure entertainment (and yes, humbling), but more than that, it's a fun way to remind them that you, too, were once small, awkward, and pretty goofy.

These snapshots tell our stories, showing how we've evolved, and they open the door to some great, unexpected conversations. Believe it or not, your kids love seeing you as a little version of yourself and discovering how you were back then. You might even hear them exclaim, "That's what I do!" or "I definitely take after you!" With every giggle and snicker, you'll feel that closeness. Let them belly-

The Muse Method: Family Activities That Bond & Brighten

laugh, point, snort, and pepper you with questions. Make it a whole event because flipping through old albums or scrolling through digital archives isn't an everyday thing. It's a little time capsule moment, so savor it.

Then, flip it and pull out their baby pictures, too. Take a walk down memory lane together, sharing those funny, sweet stories from when they were little. It's a guaranteed mood booster that takes the vibe in your home from *meh* to *magnifico*. My kids especially love seeing pictures of me at their current age; it's like I suddenly become more relatable. And hey, if that makes them more open to hearing my life lessons, well, I'm all for it!

And here's a trick that can be incredibly helpful during those inevitable teenage mood swings or exasperating moments: take a moment to yourself and flip through their baby pictures. It's a grounding reminder of just how precious, tender, and yes, extraordinary they are. This small act shifts your perspective, replacing a furrowed brow with a warm smile.

Treasure these moments. Pour all the love you can into these relationships. Before you know it, they'll be off on their own, and you'll cherish every silly and heartwarming memory you created together.

As we wrap up the Muse Methods, I hope these family activities inspire you to weave more laughter and closeness into your family's culture.

Life, like parenting, isn't all sunshine and smiles. It's messy, unpredictable, and full of curveballs that challenge us in ways we don't always see coming. This is where we shift gears.

Next up, Grab Bag Goodies, a collection of tools to empower you through life's twists and turns with confidence, turning even the toughest moments into opportunities for growth and triumph.

Chapter 9
Grab Bag Goodies!

"It's not what we do once in a while that shapes our lives. It's what we do consistently."
~Tony Robbins[12]

Let's get grabby!

Welcome to the motherlode of timeless tools, your metaphorical grab bag packed with transformative goodies! These tools are here to uplift, guide, and empower you and your kids, helping you navigate life's challenges and opportunities with adaptability and confidence. Brimming with twelve highly effective tools, this chapter is designed to make a meaningful difference in your family's life.

But don't let the abundance feel overwhelming. There's no pressure to master them all at once. Think of your grab bag as an ever-ready resource you can dip into whenever you need it. Start small. Choose one or two tools that resonate and let them work their magic. Over time, you'll find your groove, adding more tools as they naturally fit into your life.

So, what's this grab bag all about?

---

[12] Tony Robbins, Awaken the Giant Within: How to Take Immediate Control of Your Mental, Emotional, Physical, and Financial Destiny. New York, Simon & Schuster, 1992.

Parents, Grow Up!

I created the grab bag metaphor to help parents and students picture their own personal collection of power tools, tools that are always within reach to help navigate the twists and turns of life. Parenting, like life itself, is full of surprises. When you have a grab bag stocked with reliable resources, you're prepared to adapt and overcome, no matter what comes your way.

Each tool in your grab bag has the potential to create positive shifts, paving the way for a life filled with more ease, joy, and harmony. Even better, by becoming grab-bag-ready, you're equipping your kids with these tools to confidently navigate life's ups and downs.

Here's what these tools are designed to do:

- **Empower.** Boost self-confidence and remind you that you are adaptable, wise, and capable of handling any situation.
- **Guide.** Help you navigate tricky terrain and discover more productive pathways.
- **Stabilize.** Ground and center you, keeping you calm and composed no matter the challenge.
- **Illuminate.** Provide clarity on what matters most, offering strategies for wise decision-making during sensitive or turbulent times.

These tools are your faithful companions, reminding you that *you* hold the power to choose how you want the next moment to unfold. (If you need a refresher on Perpetual Arrival, flip back to Chapter 7 and soak in this phenomenal concept again.)

Remember the three life-altering decisions we make every day that shape our lives:

1. What we think
2. What we feel
3. What we do

Your grab bag helps you navigate these decisions with clarity and poise, building lasting habits that enrich your life.

Grab Bag Goodies

Often, we reach into our grab bag only when things are spiraling. Makes sense, right? When crisis strikes, we instinctively reach for help. But here's the twist: I want you to think bigger and wiser. What if you relied on your grab bag tools not just when life gets rocky but also when things are going well? Practicing during good times makes them familiar when challenges arise. As the Tony Robbins' quote at the beginning of the chapter reminds us, it's what we do consistently that shapes our lives.

Here's why you practice:

- If you've never used a certain tool before, it might not work in the middle of a crisis because you're already in freefall.
- Or, you'll grab a tool, find it awkward or clunky, and dismiss it as useless (it's not; you just haven't practiced using it).
- That's why I encourage you to reach for your grab bag tools on good days. The more you use them, the better you get. Think of it like captaining a boat; you don't become a master of the seas while docked in the harbor. You become skilled by practicing consistently. Why not get good at what's good for you? There's something exhilarating about knowing you can count on yourself no matter what. Bring it on!

Once you've mastered these tools, it's time to teach them to your kids. Empowering others begins with empowering ourselves. When you lead by example, you naturally inspire and influence your children. The goal is to make your grab bag tools a lasting habit, not a last resort. The more you use them, the more intuitive they become, always riding shotgun, ready when you need them.

Now, what happens if your kids skip using their grab bag? Brace yourself. Imagine your phone blowing up with texts from your anxious, overwhelmed kid—nonstop crises about friend drama, tough professors, breakups, laundry pileups, or the existential dread of adulting. Without a grab bag, they'll be flailing, and guess who they'll turn to for rescue? That's right; you are always on call.

But if they've been taught to use a grab bag, they'll know how to flip the switch from chaos to calm, from freakout to focused. They'll stand on their own two feet, navigate life with confidence, and create the life they want without sweating every bump in the road.

True story...

I know several parents who are their adult children's everything—confidant, scheduler, nutritionist, therapist, career counselor, personal shopper, caregiver, rescuer, and, ultimately, wing-clipper. It's something I've seen firsthand more times than I can count.

Here's one specific example I'd like to share: During a coaching session with a mom, her young adult son texted her, no joke, twenty-three times and called once. With all the pings, dings, and rings going off, I thought it had to be an emergency. But no. Her son was spiraling because he couldn't find a specific spice for a marinade recipe. Yes, twenty-three texts and a call…about a spice. And no, the issue wasn't resolved by the end of our session.

You can probably guess what we focused on in our next session. And absolutely no judgment here. We both laughed about it and were actually thrilled it happened in real time. It made the issue impossible to JED (M8 #7: Justify, Excuse, or Defend), shining a spotlight on what needed to change. That moment became the catalyst for a breakthrough and the start of real growth for them both.

Here's the truth: Life is an inside job. Everything we need, we already have within us. It's all about recognizing that our self-worth, mindset, and belief in our abilities shape everything. These internal qualities influence the choices we make every single day, moment by moment.

Teach your kids that they're responsible for the quality of their lives. (Cue M8 #3: If It Is to Be, It Is Up to Me!) By nurturing these inner strengths, they'll grow into capable and content individuals who take charge of their lives from the inside out and create something they're proud of.

So, how do we fortify these internal strengths? That's where the grab bag comes in. Let's unpack these goodies and discover how they can help you and your family flourish!

The Magnificent 8 (M8)

You know the M8 well. It's been the steady thread running through every chapter, showcasing its undeniable power. Now, it takes its rightful place as the ultimate grab bag goodie, and for good reason. The M8 is the ultimate powerhouse for life, earning its spot as my number one go-to tool.

At its core, the M8 is your steadfast inner foundation, the bedrock for building a life filled with wisdom, strength, harmony, and joy. Mastering the M8 transforms your perspective, illuminates wiser choices, promotes kindness, and nurtures warmth, all while boosting your productivity and enriching your relationships. It's your toolkit for every moment of every day. Need a refresher? Revisit its magnificence in Chapter 2.

1. **Put Your Oxygen Mask on First.** Your breath is your life force. Use Dr. Weil's 4-7-8 breathing technique to soothe, center, calm, or energize.
2. **Begin with the End in Mind.** Zoom out to see the bigger picture. What outcome are you desiring? What's the goal?
3. **If It Is to Be, It Is Up to Me.** You are 100 percent responsible for the quality of your life. Own it. Be empowered by it!
4. **Desire and Discipline: The Dynamic Duo.** This dynamic duo is the fuel behind every accomplishment. Desire ignites motivation; discipline gets results.
5. **The 4 A's: Awareness, Acknowledge, Assess, Action.** These four steps create clarity and insight for a wiser path forward.
6. **Pain of Regret or Pain of Discipline.** Every decision comes with a cost. Which pain are you willing to endure? Choose wisely.
7. **JED is Dead!** No more Justifying, Excusing, or Defending. These reveal insecurities and distractions that block growth. Stop skirting the issue.
8. **Humor.** Bring humor, levity, and joy wherever and whenever possible. Lighten up, be lighthearted, and laugh (a lot).

Parents, Grow Up!

The 5-Fold-Why

Ah, the 5-Fold-Why, an oldie but such a goodie. It's my trusted ally for navigating life's little emotional hiccups or landmines, whether with my kids, clients, or myself. Think of it like your favorite playlist on shuffle: it feels good, always hits the right notes, and somehow makes every situation better. Whether your teen is upset because their phone died mid-Snap streak, your young adult is spiraling over not hearing back from their professor fast enough, or you're losing it over spilling your latte in the center console of your car, the 5-Fold-Why helps you cut through the noise and get to the heart of the matter.

The process is simple: ask *why* five times, or as many licks as it takes to get to the center of a Tootsie Pop (a nod to the iconic 1969 commercial), peeling back a layer with each question to uncover the core issue and discover what's really bothering them. It's like peeling an onion, but without the tears (most of the time). Each *why* brings you closer to the truth, which is often much smaller or more manageable than it first seemed. Let's be honest; the first answer is usually like tossing a big log onto a cold fire. It's probably impulsive, over the top, but you know it won't catch. The 5-Fold-Why is the kindling, gently coaxing the real flames (the conversation) to life. And the best part? It's curious, non-judgmental, illuminating, and, dare I say, kind of fun.

Here's a 5-Fold-Why in action:

Imagine your college-aged son or daughter calling you in the middle of the day, sounding stressed.

You:	Hey, you sound really upset. What's going on?
Them:	I'm so angry. I totally bombed my chemistry exam.
You:	Oh no, I'm sorry. Why do you think you bombed?
Them:	Because I wasn't as prepared as I could have been.
You:	I see. Why do you think you weren't prepared?
Them:	Because I've been trying to be more social.
You:	Why are you feeling the need to be more social?

Them:	Because I'm too shy and don't know how to make friends.
You:	Why are you feeling so shy and unsure?
Them:	Because it seems like everyone has their group of friends but me. I feel so disconnected and lonely.

Insight: This conversation started with frustration over a failed exam, but as you gently peeled back the layers, the real issue emerged, which is loneliness and a sense of disconnection. College can be tricky to navigate, especially when it feels like everyone else has found their people. What initially seemed like an academic struggle turned out to be a reflection of a deeper emotional challenge.

By asking why with curiosity and care, you uncovered what was really bothering them. It wasn't just about chemistry; it was about feeling isolated and shy, which affected everything from studying to their overall well-being. Now, instead of focusing solely on grades, you can offer the emotional support they really need. You might help them explore ways to build social connections, easing their loneliness, which in turn can lift their spirits and improve their academic focus.

The 5-Fold-Why revealed the bigger picture: they weren't just struggling with a subject; they were struggling to belong, yearning for real connection. It's a powerful reminder that what we see on the surface—a tough class or a rough day—is often just the tip of the iceberg. Beneath it can lie deeper, unspoken worries that need our understanding, patience, and compassion. By digging deeper, you're not just addressing a problem; you're helping them feel heard and teaching them how to uncover the heart of the matter instead of skimming the surface.

The Yep and Nope of Control

Oh boy, let's talk about *control*. It's one of those loaded words in the parenting playbook that can make or break your sanity. Let's face it: No one throws around "controlling" as a compliment. It's more like a giant neon sign flashing, "Warning: Insecurity Ahead!" And trust me, I've been there. Both of my kids have described me as controlling when reflecting on their childhood. Regretfully, they're absolutely right, big time.

I was a master at JEDing my need to control, convincing myself it was for their own good. In reality, my iron grip was just a mask for my own insecurities, fears, and unresolved wounds. I've grown a lot since those days, and, dear God, I diligently continue to work on this. Props and gratitude to the M8, I've learned (and keep learning) to hold myself accountable and choose a wiser path forward. It's a tough one to kick completely, but I'm up for the challenge because, hey, tenacity is one of my superpowers!

Back in my control-freak days, my need for control showed up everywhere. Feeding the pets? Had to be done my way, on the schedule I deemed right. The result? I became the full-time, on-duty zookeeper. And let's not even get started on how to clean the litter boxes. Doing the dishes and loading the dishwasher? Forget it. If it wasn't done exactly as I wanted, you'd be booted out, and I'd take over. You can probably guess how that turned out: the dishes became my domain, all while I sent the unintended message that I didn't trust my kids to do it right. Oof.

Here's the twist I didn't see coming: controlling people are often the ones most out of control. Sound familiar? My need for control was rooted in my own chaos, a dumpster fire of insecurities from years past. Facing that mess head-on has been one of the hardest yet most rewarding journeys of my life. There's no finish line for self-improvement. Letting go of control is a daily decision, but the freedom it brings is worth every bit of effort.

Now, don't misunderstand me. There are times when parental control is absolutely necessary, like when your toddler tries to snack on crayons or your teen thinks curfews are optional. But I'm talking about the sneaky ways control creeps into everyday moments, impacting how we see ourselves, our relationships, and our quality of life.

Grab Bag Goodies

The Good, the Bad, and the Real Work

Before you can teach your kids about control, you must face your own relationship with it. Yes, this might mean confronting your own inner dumpster fire, whether it's raging or smoldering. And yes, the process of putting it out can be absolutely exhausting, messy, and quite humbling. When you release what you cannot control, you'll experience sweet liberation. Let that freedom ring!

This simple yet impactful exercise helps you clearly see what's within your control and what isn't, freeing up your energy to focus on what truly matters.

Control Exercise:

1. Take a sheet of paper and draw two columns.
2. On the left, list everything you *can* control. On the right, write down what you *can't*.
3. Be honest. No JEDing.

This exercise is designed to help you identify what you can and can't control, freeing up energy for what truly matters. Remember, it's not about making a quick list and calling it a day. When you see the categories listed below, I want you to dig deeper into each one.

Don't skim the surface or lump everything together with, "I only have control over myself, that's obvious." That mindset will rob you of the sweet liberation this exercise can bring. Instead, take the time to get specific and personal. Get into the nitty-gritty of each category. To guide you, I've included examples of what I mean when I say, "go deeper."

And remember, the M8 is your trusty ally in getting this done and done right. These tools can help you stay focused, intentional, and honest as you work through each layer. Ready to do the work and feel the reward? Here are some examples:

Within My Control

- **Quality of my thoughts.** Instead of thinking, "This is impossible, I'll never figure it out," reframe it to: "This is

tough, but I can break it into smaller steps and make progress."
- **My choice of words.** When a heated moment arises, choose phrases like, "I hear you, and I'd like us to find a solution together," rather than blurting out, "You never listen to me!"
- **My responses and reactions.** Instead of snapping at your child for leaving their shoes in the doorway again, take a breath (M8 #1) and calmly say, "I'd love for your shoes to live in your closet. I don't think they like being stepped on." (M8 #8, Humor)

Outside My Control

- **What other people say.** If someone is being rude, remember that's their "stuff." It gives you great insight into who they are. You can't control their narrative.
- **Other people's reactions.** If someone's reaction isn't what you expected, observe, don't absorb. You have zero control over what comes out of their mouth.
- **Other people's decisions.** You can guide, suggest, or even strongly encourage, but ultimately, the decisions they make are theirs alone, just as yours are.

When you step back and take a good look, it becomes clear: The only things you truly have control over are what you think, feel, say, and do. That's it. And that's more than enough. Again, life is an inside job. Once you grasp that you can't control anyone or anything outside of yourself, it's like slipping off a pair of shoes that are two sizes too small. *Ahhh*...instant relief. You'll feel like you can finally let out a deep, overdue exhale and regain that bounce in your step.

Grab Bag Goodies

The Control Chart

Within My Control	Outside of My Control
• Quality of my thoughts • My choice of words • My responses & reactions • My attitude • The boundaries I create • My decisions • My routines • My choice of friends • My self-worth	• What other people say • Other people's reactions • Other people's responses • Other people's attitudes • Other people's decisions • Other people's expectations • The future • The weather • Traffic

Once you've written down your list of what's within your control and what's not, tear it down the middle. Keep the *Within My Control* side somewhere visible, a constant reminder of where to focus your energy. As for the *Outside My Control* list? Let it go. Burn it, shred it, or toss it in the trash. The method doesn't matter as much as the act itself. Destroying it is a declaration that you will no longer carry what you cannot control. Much like decluttering a space, this process clears out mental and emotional junk, making room for what truly matters: your peace of mind.

As a parent, this exercise is a paradigm shifter. Deep down, we all know what we can and cannot control. Yet somehow, we still manage to shoulder the weight of our kids, partners, families, friends, and coworkers, and hey! Why not throw the state of the world on there, too? It's exhausting. Worse, it blocks our inner peace and creates unnecessary stress—both within ourselves and in our relationships.

So, do it. Shred that *Outside My Control* list. Kick off those too-tight shoes and go barefoot for a bit. Let yourself feel grounded, lighter, and freer. This exercise is one of the first tools I share with parents and students because the shift is so immediate. The relief is real.

Equanimity: The Holy Grail

Have you heard the word "equanimity" before? If not, I'm thrilled to introduce it to you. And trust me, by the time we're done, you won't just know the word; you'll want to embrace it, live it, and make it a cornerstone of your family's culture. Why? Because equanimity is both a soothing companion and a powerful compass. It guides you through life's challenges, helping you stay in harmony mentally and emotionally.

Equanimity is that serene state of mind that lets you handle life's curveballs with poise and grace. It allows you to cultivate a deep sense of inner peace, even amidst chaos. It grounds you when everything around you feels uncertain. Here's the best part: equanimity is one of the most transformative superpowers you can develop. It's not just about keeping the peace within your family; it's about maintaining your own inner calm no matter what's happening outside you. Imagine navigating life's rollercoaster with composure and a deep sense of stability. That's the magic of equanimity. It creates a state of peace and tranquility.

And like all meaningful pursuits, it requires effort, and Desire and Discipline (M8 #4). But equanimity isn't a passing mood or fleeting emotion; it's a way of being.

How to Cultivate Equanimity

One of the most effective ways to develop this inner superpower is through visualization. When your mind enters a space of calm and peace, your body naturally follows like a faithful and obedient companion. (Our body and brain are extraordinary. Use them to serve *you*! Cue M8 #3: If It Is to Be, It Is Up to Me.)

To begin, think of a place, person, pet, or memory that brings you comfort and relaxation. Picture it vividly:

- What do you see?
- What colors surround you?
- What sounds fill the air?
- What scent lingers?
- What do you feel?

Engage all your senses until it feels real, as though you're truly there. That's the magic of visualization. Your mind creates the experience, and your body responds with calm and peace. The best part? You don't need a yoga studio, a retreat, or even thirty minutes. It can take as little as five minutes or as long as you need. Whether you're brushing your teeth, pumping gas, or baking cookies, you can turn inward, visualize, and guide yourself to that calm, grounded place.

If you're looking for inspiration, think of a mountain. A mountain withstands storms, droughts, and fires with quiet strength and resilience. It endures and adapts. Equanimity is your mountain. *Be the mountain.*

Why Equanimity Matters

Equanimity isn't just a nice-to-have; it's essential. It deserves your reverence because it's the quiet strength that lives deep within you, waiting to be awakened and nurtured. Once you tap into it, you'll wonder how you ever lived without it.

This same quiet strength resides within your kids, ready to be cultivated. Teaching them to connect with their inner calm is a grab bag essential, especially in this age of anxiety. Guiding them to discover equanimity will transform how they face challenges, granting them access to a lifelong source of calm.

Helping your kids make equanimity a permanent seat at their soul's table might just be one of the most profound gifts you ever give them.

Be the Otter

Building on the power of visualization (as we did with equanimity), let me introduce another client favorite: the Be the Otter visualization. First, let's distinguish between the two.

The equanimity visualization taps into what's already within us—our inner calm and quiet strength. It's about accessing a state of being that resides in us at all times.

Be the Otter, on the other hand, is more situational. It's a quick and playful reset designed for those moments when emotions run high and you need to regain balance fast. Think of it as a short, sweet invitation to catch your breath, relax your heart, and center yourself on the spot.

Now, let's glide into the otter's world. Picture her floating serenely on her back, forefeet resting gently on her belly. She breathes calmly, gazing up at the sky as she lets go of tension, basking in the moment with ease. The otter invites you to pause, exhale, and float right alongside her.

When you or your children feel a wave of strong emotions—irritation, sadness, anxiety, or overwhelm—take a moment to Be the Otter. Close your eyes and step into her peaceful presence. As you visualize, let your body respond: feel worries melting, shoulders softening, heartbeat slowing, and stress floating away. Welcome in the calm of the otter.

This practice is very comforting, whether used after a tough conversation, during moments of overwhelm, or even as part of a bedtime routine (it is especially soothing for kids!). The otter reminds us that, no matter the situation, we can create space for calm and relaxation.

Visualization is one of the most effective tools you can carry. When your mind drifts toward soothing imagery, your body naturally follows. So, next time life feels heavy, Be the Otter. Float, breathe, and let go. Let her quiet magic transform your moment.

Wishing Your Bed Was Already Made!

(Go on, sing "Manic Monday" by The Bangles!) Think about it: the moment you make your bed, you've already accomplished something. Even if the rest of the room looks like a tornado passed through, you're one step ahead. Who doesn't love the feeling of slipping into a made bed after a long day? It's the ultimate home-sweet-home moment.

Your bed is the focal point of your room, so why not make it the MVP of your day?

It's often the little things that have the biggest impact on your mood, outlook, and productivity. Take the kitchen sink, for example. Facing a mountain of dirty dishes first thing in the morning? Ugh. Talk about starting the day already feeling behind. A messy space can mess with your mindset.

When your surroundings are chaotic, your life feels chaotic, too. Your environment reflects how you're managing (or not managing) the day-to-day. Keeping things tidy isn't just about appearances; it's about how that action makes you feel. An organized space offers peace of mind and gives you that deep, satisfying exhale, setting the stage for a focused and productive day.

On the flip side: a cluttered, messy space? That's an energy drain. It's a mental drain ("I really need to clean this…"), an emotional drain (feeling overwhelmed by the mess), and a physical drain (moving piles just to find a spot to work or locate something you swear is in there somewhere). These energy leaks spill over into your entire day and impact the people around you.

Over the years of working with families, I've created a little starter kit—my top quick clean-ups, which I call "The Big Three." These simple, effective clean-ups focus on the areas in your home that matter most: the ones everyone notices first and where you spend the most time.

Tackling these areas won't just make your home look more put together; it'll give you great satisfaction. Teaching your kids to take responsibility for their spaces now prepares them for the day they'll manage their own homes (and clean up after themselves).

Here are The Big Three—simple, daily wins you (and your kids) can easily knock out:

1. **Make your bed.** Seriously, just do it. The smile you'll have climbing into bed later is worth those two minutes.
2. **Do the dishes.** A clean sink really does equal a calmer mind.
3. **Wipe down the bathroom sink and counter.** Stash some antibacterial wipes nearby for quick cleanups.

Simple, right? The Big Three aren't monumental tasks. They're small habits with big rewards. These daily wins bring calm and order to your home while teaching kids valuable life skills. When kids take responsibility for their spaces, they build self-competence and learn to trust in their ability to care for themselves and their surroundings.

The Big Three can easily be introduced as early as kindergarten. I'll admit, I came a bit late to this party; I didn't start implementing it with my kids until high school. Better late than never, right? Starting earlier allows kids to grow into more responsibilities over time, building their independence along the way.

So, start today. Whether you're setting an example or teaching your kids, let The Big Three work their magic. These small steps lead to big changes.

Zip It, Skip It, Flip It!

One of my secret superpowers? Crafting catchy quips that stick. These little gems (like a jingle) pop into my mind at just the right time, and they always inspire action. Over the years, these creative phrases have helped me recenter. They have guided me toward much wiser decisions, especially with my kids. One of my all-time favorites? *Zip It, Skip It, Flip It!*

This simple, memorable mantra came to me during a moment of frustration when I was struggling to listen and trying not to blurt out regretful remarks to my kids. All I could hear in my head was, *Jill, zip it*! And just like that, the phrase was born, saving my relationships one zip at a time.

Zip It!

Sometimes the best thing you can do is…nothing. Take a breath and just *listen*. Especially with kids, they're usually not looking for advice or solutions. As the saying goes, "Kids need to be listened to more than they need to be talked to." They want your presence. A safe space to vent, crumble, or be vulnerable.

There's a big difference between vulnerability and complaining, and if you pause, you'll feel the difference. Resist the urge to jump in with words. Zip it. Be still. Let them ride the wave of emotion. It will eventually settle while you stand by with warmth and a non-judgmental presence. Listen loudly. It's what they need.

Skip It!

Then there are those times when you feel the urge to chime in, whether it's to add your two cents, share an opinion, or scratch that itch to push their buttons, even though deep down you know it won't help. I catch myself all the time, ready to jump in, but then I stop and remind myself, *Jill, skip it*!

Instead of fueling friction, let it go. Skip the power struggle, the last word, or the need to prove a point. You'll be amazed at what happens next: Tension fades, and space opens up for understanding and connection. By skipping the temptation to engage, you're effectively stepping back, and that small shift can feel like a weight lifted for both you and your kids.

Flip It!

When you feel a conversation heading for the danger zone, whether with family, friends, or anyone, it's time to *Flip It*, gently shift the focus with curiosity or a sprinkle of humor. Flip the topic, redirect the energy, and guide things out of the danger zone.

It's a subtle yet effective way to lighten the mood and keep the connection intact. Sometimes, all it takes is a well-timed joke, a clever observation, or a thoughtful question to turn things around.

Sometimes, you'll need just one of these strategies; other times, all three. But together, they're mighty. *Zip It, Skip It, Flip It* improves conversations, diffuses conflict, strengthens relationships, and just might save Thanksgiving dinner from going south. Here's your challenge: before you speak, pause and ask yourself, *Zip it? Skip it? Or Flip it?* Are you adding or taking away? Will your words lift someone up? Or bring them down? Choose thoughtfully. Make your words matter.

This tool works wonders, especially during emotionally charged conversations. Keep *Zip It, Skip It, Flip It!* in your front pocket, and you'll cultivate healthier, more respectful, and more enjoyable relationships, not just with your kids but with everyone around you.

Remember, you're the leader. Lead with care and a generous dose of humor! (M8 #8)

Energy Is Everything

Ever heard the saying, "Your energy introduces you before you even speak"? It's spot on. Energy is our invisible signature, our life force, the thing people sense before a single word is exchanged. Think about it: how often have you picked up on someone's vibe without knowing a thing about them? Whether you're standing in line at the store, being greeted at a restaurant, or spending time with your kids, energy is always at play. It can lift the entire mood or drag it down. Ever said, "Wow, I love her energy!" or "I'm not liking his vibe."? That's because energy can make things feel in flow or blocked, good or bad. It's a major contributor to how we feel about ourselves and how others feel in our presence.

Your energy is your essence. It shapes your well-being and the way you move through the world. It touches every part of your life: your thoughts, decisions, relationships, and how you navigate life's twists and turns. That's why keeping your energy healthy is so important. This means being aware of the quality of your thoughts, feelings, and actions, so they are in sync with the person you are proud to be. Over time, emotional and mental clutter can weigh you down, cloud your mind, and block the flow of your energy. Before you can uplift others, your own energy needs regular care and cleansing. So how do you do that? It starts with consistent deep cleaning, so to speak, through self-awareness, introspection, or simply pausing to reset. For example, your energy might feel drained if your home is in disarray—daunting piles of clutter can weigh on you mentally, making it hard to feel at ease. At work, your energy could be blocked if you're doing something out of alignment with your values, leaving you heavy-hearted and disappointed for not staying true to what you believe in. Or maybe your energy feels strained in your relationship with your kids because your expectations aren't being met, creating frustration.

When you take the time to recognize where and why your energy is being affected, you can start to unblock it and get it flowing again. For instance, pick a weekend to tackle those piles and get your home organized. You'll be amazed by how quickly your energy gets back in flow. Look for opportunities to align your work with what fills your heart, whether through volunteering, pursuing a passion project, or simply finding meaning in your day-to-day tasks. And with your kids, take time to reassess your expectations. Use the M8's tools to stay aligned with your desired outcomes.

Regular care and cleansing of your energy involves tuning in, adjusting, and making choices that restore your flow and sense of well-being. This practice is as important as anything else on your to-do list. When you take care of your inner world, you radiate positive energy outward, uplifting yourself and everyone around you.

Maintaining good energy isn't only about cleansing; it's about managing it wisely. Forget time management for a moment and focus on energy management. Time may be finite, but the quality of your energy is what really makes the hours in your day count. Instead of stressing about how little time you have, ask yourself, *How can I optimize my energy to make the most of this time?*

Parents, Grow Up!

Protecting and preserving your energy is essential to feeling healthy. Make it a habit to check your energy—both its levels and its quality. While life can be unpredictable—with sleepless nights, work stress, or unexpected happenings—your body has a natural rhythm. Are you a midday warrior? A night owl? Learn your energy patterns. If mornings aren't your jam, don't force yourself into high-stakes tasks before 10 a.m. Schedule more demanding tasks during your peak energy hours, whether that's late-night creative bursts, afternoon meetings, or an evening workout.

Bring this awareness into family life. Observe the energy rhythms of your kids. Maybe they're early risers who peter out by midafternoon or night owls who come alive at dark. Understanding their natural flow can create more harmony and productivity.

We all hit low-battery zones, which make activities or tasks that are mentally, emotionally, or physically demanding feel impossible. The key is knowing how to recharge. Refueling is essential, whether that happens from a walk, good music, a favorite meal, or connecting with someone who lifts your spirit. And remember, sleep isn't negotiable for kids. Their growing bones, developing brains, and overall health depend on consistent, quality rest.

Energy ebbs and flows. That's normal. Knowing your family's rhythms allows you to choose the right moments for meaningful conversations, big decisions, or simply recharging. When you're in sync with your family's energy, life feels smoother, and positive outcomes are more likely.

How are these grab bag goodies landing for you so far? Can you sense the potential impact they can have? Don't let the variety feel overwhelming. Let them support and empower you. Start small: choose one or two tools that resonate with you and begin weaving them into your daily life. As you grow more confident, gradually introduce others at your own pace. Then, keep the momentum going as you continue adding more goodies to your grab bag!

Deliberate Acts of Goodness

I love acts of goodness, whether they're random, impulsive, or deliberate. When people ask me, "What do you believe in?" My answer is simple: kindness. Kindness is my jam, my belief system.

I'm a passionate advocate for deliberate acts of goodness. Forget the mindset of "What have you done for me lately?" Instead, I believe in personal accountability: I'm fully responsible for my own happiness, health, and sense of worth. One of my core principles is "If It Is to Be, It Is Up to Me" (M8 #3). And the quality of my life, as well as the quality of my character, is 100 percent my responsibility.

One of the most fulfilling ways to feel purposeful (and to make a difference) is to give of ourselves. When we shift our focus from me, me, me to extending kindness to others, something extraordinary happens: we generate positive energy, deepen our connections, and experience a sense of satisfaction that comes only from making someone else's day a little brighter.

Deliberate acts of goodness don't have to be grand to matter. Spend quality time with your pet or foster an animal in need of love and care. Share apples from your backyard tree with a neighbor. Bake cookies for a friend. Surprise a co-worker with their favorite coffee. Take a moment to sincerely ask someone, "How are you?" and truly listen to their answer. Pick up trash during your daily walk to show respect for our planet. These simple gestures are proof that every kindness counts.

In today's fast-paced world, deliberate acts of goodness are more essential than ever. Too often, we're glued to our screens—heads down, distracted, and disconnected—missing the moments that make life meaningful. Eye contact, a smile shared with a stranger, a hearty laugh with a friend, a genuine conversation, or simply offering your full presence are acts that fulfill what we all deeply crave: to matter, to belong, to feel seen and loved. Invite your kids to choose their unique ways to spread kindness. By intentionally practicing deliberate acts of goodness, you create meaningful memories and weave them into the tapestry of your life. These deliberate acts not only enrich your experiences but also reflect the character you carry into the world. Shifting from *me* to *we* is deeply gratifying. The ripple effect of intentional acts of kindness stretches far beyond the initial act, often touching lives in ways we may never see.

As a family, you can make deliberate acts of goodness a regular practice and an integral part of your family's culture.

The Happy Sound of Healing

Humming is as old as humanity itself. Across cultures and generations, it has served as a universal expression of joy, relaxation, and even healing. But did you know that humming isn't just a happy habit? It's also a powerful wellness tool. Humming strengthens the immune system, helps the body heal, fights off germs, and lifts our moods. Think about it: Have you ever seen a grumpy person humming? I challenge you to find one! People hum when they're content, when a catchy tune is stuck in their head, or when they're simply enjoying the moment. So, if you're like me and sometimes just can't stop humming a random song on a loop in your brain, appreciate that it might actually be doing you more good than you realize!

Humming works wonders by creating vibrational resonance in the body. These vibrations balance and energize you from within, triggering a natural relaxation response that reduces stress and promotes calm. It's been shown to positively influence the parasympathetic nervous system—the part of your brain that tells your body, "Hey, chill out"—which not only helps reduce stress but also supports digestion, regulates breathing, and boosts overall wellness. In other words, humming is like a wellness hack you didn't know you had. Whether you're feeling great or going through a rough patch, it's a tool you'll want to keep in your grab bag. Sound healing is an incredible tool for self-care, and humming is one of the easiest and most joyful ways to experience its benefits. While there's plenty of scientific talk about how sound waves and vibrations promote healing, you don't need to dive into the jargon to feel the difference.

You don't have to understand every detail of vibrational resonance to experience the benefits of humming.

Humming is a simple, natural, and joyful practice that can make a real difference in your family's life. As parents, you have the power to model this practice for your kids, showing them how small, intentional habits can have a big impact on mental and physical well-being. By weaving humming into your daily routine, you model for your kids a lifelong tool to de-stress, feel better, and stay balanced, even during the busiest times.

Make humming a part of your everyday rhythm, whether you're doing dishes, folding laundry, cooking, walking the dog, gardening, or driving. Let it become a happy and healing habit. It's fun, it's free, and it can lift your mood in an instant.

The Best Way to Tuck Yourself In

The word *gratitude* is everywhere these days, but let's not let its true depth get lost in the buzz. Gratitude is more than a trend—and more than a mantra—it's a transformative way to live. As the saying goes, "Gratitude makes optimism sustainable." It's that quiet, steady anchor in our ever-changing world.

One of the best times to center yourself in gratitude is right before bed. This is your moment to let the stress of the day melt away and give your mind and body the rest they deserve. I call this simple yet powerful ritual "Goodnight Gratitudes." There are no rules. It can take less than a minute or as long as you need. As you settle in for the night, switch off your devices, close your eyes, and take a deep breath. Reflect on three things you're grateful for. These don't need to be life-changing, just genuine. The goal is to train your mind to notice and appreciate the good in your day. As you do, feel how your body relaxes and your mind softens.

Here are three areas to guide your reflections:

1. **Something about yourself.** Think of a small win from your today. Maybe you handled a tough moment gracefully or managed to keep your cool in traffic. Even the little victories

matter! It could be, "I'm proud I didn't hit 'reply all' on that email," or "I'm thankful for those three snoozes. I really needed the rest."
2. **Something about your family.** Whether it's your partner or kids, focus on those moments of connection. Maybe it's, "I'm thankful I won rock-paper-scissors and didn't have to empty the dishwasher," or "I'm grateful my family members are foodies, so I can count on satisfying grub sessions."
3. **Something about Mother Earth.** Reflect on nature's gifts. Maybe it's "I'm grateful for the squirrels in the yard. They are great morning entertainment!" Or "I'm grateful for the vibrant hydrangeas outside. They always make me smile."

You can do this practice alone, with your partner, or with your kids. It's a beautiful way to bond and reflect on the little things, the moments that often go unnoticed but mean so much. This simple ritual ends your day on a sweet note, shifting your focus from grumpy to grateful.

Resilient by Design

A Harvard-trained psychologist, Dr. Cortney S. Warren, PhD, shared a common trait among emotionally strong and resilient people: they use empowering phrases to shape their mindset and navigate life's inevitable challenges.[13] These simple statements become part of their everyday language, helping them face adversity with confidence and adaptability.

When I share these nine transformative statements with my clients, the reaction is often the same: "Yeah, I know them." But here's the thing: Knowing them isn't enough. The real power lies in believing them and living them until they become second nature.

For the most resilient people, these statements aren't occasional tools like Chapstick pulled out on a ski trip. They're ingrained habits

---

[13] https://www.cnbc.com/2023/08/06/harvard-psychologist-if-you-use-any-of-these-phrases-you-are-more-emotionally-resilient-than-most.html

that create a mental framework to support them through life's ups and downs. Imagine equipping your kids with this framework. Teaching these statements early gives them lifelong tools to handle challenges with grit and grace.

Resilient people don't react to hardship. They intentionally shape their responses. They allow themselves to feel and process their emotions, then quickly focus on what they can control and how to keep moving forward.

Here are the nine resilient statements:

1. "I can get through this." A reminder of your inner strength and ability to persevere, no matter how hard it gets.
2. "I refuse to be a victim." Challenges may arise, and your responses to them can define you. Choose empowerment over defeat.
3. "Life is hard." Acknowledging this truth helps you face challenges head-on and adapt rather than resist.
4. "This too shall pass." Even the darkest storms are temporary. They don't last forever.
5. "What can I learn from this?" Life's toughest moments often teach the greatest lessons if we're open to learning them.
6. "I need some time." It's okay to step back, breathe, and give yourself space to think, feel, and act.
7. "I still have things to be grateful for." Gratitude exists even in the hardest of times. Look for it, and you'll find it.
8. "It is what it is." Acceptance can be freeing. Let go of what you can't control and focus on what you can. Keep moving forward.
9. "I'm letting this go." Holding onto pain or grudges only weighs you down. Release it. Onward and upward!

Roll Resilience into Your Family's Values

Share these statements with your children and talk about which ones resonate most. The earlier they embrace this resilient mindset, the better equipped they'll be to navigate life's inevitable challenges with adaptability and confidence.

These nine statements are more than just words—they're a roadmap to a stronger, more confident life. Start incorporating them into your daily routine and your family's values. Together, you'll create a family environment that values strength, growth, and empowerment, no matter what life throws your way. After all, *it is what it is*! (I use them every chance I get!)

With this final tool, your grab bag is complete and filled with treasures to support and empower you both as a person and as a parent. Putting these tools into action will naturally teach your kids how to navigate life with greater ease, wisdom, and joy. These grab bag goodies are always there for you, ready to reframe your narrative, elevate your life, and deepen your family's connections. At the end of the day, it all comes down to you. You're in control. You choose what you think, feel, and do. These three decisions? They shape who you are and the life you're creating. If it is to be, it's up to *you*!

Conclusion: Yes, You're Ready!

"Motivation is what gets you started. Habit is what keeps you going."
~Jim Rohn

Congratulations! You've made it! Welcome to the starting line of an ever-evolving, ever-empowered life.

Picture me doing backflips, cartwheels, and tossing glittering confetti in the air because this moment is monumental! You've reached a milestone worth celebrating, and I couldn't be prouder of the journey you've taken.

Here's the truth: You now hold everything you need to create a solid foundation for yourself and your family. One that is strong, stable, and ready to support you with every step forward. You've shown up, committed to your personal growth, and invested in strengthening your family's relationships. Now you have a system, an actionable plan, and a treasure chest packed with timeless tools to serve you and your family.

Think of this book as your ultimate toolkit that is designed to help you become a parent of influence and inspiration, a legendary listener, and the architect of an enriching family culture.

But here's the thing: knowledge is only the first step. Now, it's time to transform what you've learned into action. The kind of action that builds momentum, creates traction, and propels you from knowing to doing. The kind of action that takes you from thinking to creating. As the saying goes, "Well done is better than well said."

This is just the beginning. You've got this. You're ready.

Review, Reflect, and Reset

As we wrap up, let's revisit the heart of this journey. Below is a chapter-by-chapter review to help you align your heart and head, keeping the insights you've gained front and center. Throughout this book, I've emphasized that there's no magic formula for positive change. The only reasons you won't get the results you want are simple:

1. You don't believe it.
2. You don't do it.
3. You don't stick with it.

That's it—belief, action, and consistency. These are the secret ingredients to creating lasting habits. Get those right, and the results will follow. Remember Desire and Discipline: The Dynamic Duo (M8 #4)—together, they fuel transformation.

Use this conclusion chapter as your trusty guide, a nudge to revisit the chapters when you need a reminder or reinforcement. And don't let perfection trip you up. Forget those unattainable expectations. Life is unpredictable, and family is complicated. No tool, hack, or shortcut will entirely erase tough days or challenges. But these tools can help you turn a bad day into a better one, a poor choice into a wise decision, a spiraling mind into a centered state, or a difficult conversation into a productive dialogue.

It all starts with you. As I profess: "When you're well, the whole world benefits, especially your family." This truth matters. You are your family's first and most important leader. The culture you create becomes the ecosystem where your family will either flourish or wither.

You hold immense power as a parent. And with great power comes great responsibility. Handle it with care, humility, and, yes, a big dose of humor (M8 #8); you'll need it!

Conclusion: Yes, You're Ready

Every chapter in this book was built with intention and builds upon the previous one. By adopting all the strategies discussed, you can create a stable and lasting framework for your family. You've got this.

Chapter 1 Recap: Getting Real, Real Quick

Chapter 1 invites you to stop searching for answers outside yourself. *You are the answer you've been seeking.* You are the solution to your well-being and the key to your family's wholeness. Remember, you can't change your children—or anyone else, for that matter. True transformation begins with changing yourself.

This chapter challenges you to confront who you are, why you are the way you are, and how you show up in the world. Are you unintentionally fracturing your family's foundation? Be brutally honest about what you're contributing to—or contaminating in—your family's ecosystem. Avoid complacency. Instead, dive deep into the Many Layers of You, exploring how each one shapes your family's environment.

Once you've taken this honest look, turn your focus to the core eight elements of your family's culture, the heart of your home. These include:

1. Family Values
2. Family Traditions
3. Family Rituals
4. Family Beliefs
5. Family Attitudes
6. Home Environment
7. Family Priorities
8. Family Goals

As the leader of your family, remember that none of these elements are set in stone. You are constantly evolving and learning—a true student of life. Growth requires courage, adaptability, and flexibility. Stay open as you refine or redefine these components. Don't let pride or fear stand in the way of becoming your best self.

Parents, Grow Up!

Recognizing the need for improvement is the first step toward meaningful change.

Chapter 2 Recap: The Magnificent 8!

It's go time—tool time—*action time*. The moment to move forward with purpose has arrived. These eight foundational principles form a solid framework to combat negativity, procrastination, and stagnation. Each one can transform you—whether as an individual, a parent, or a friend. Any of the M8 principles can elevate relationships, enhance decisions, and change the trajectory of circumstances for the better.

Improving your relationships begins with improving yourself. Read that again—and keep reading it until you believe it 100 percent.

Allow the M8 to be your lifelong companion, keeping you and your family supported and empowered:

1. **Put Your Oxygen Mask on First.** Prioritize your well-being. Start with Dr. Weil's 4-7-8 breathing technique to calm and ground yourself. You can't take care of others effectively if you don't take care of yourself.
2. **Begin with the End in Mind.** Visualize the outcome you want. Clarity of your goal will drive your actions.
3. **If It Is to Be, It Is Up to Me.** You are 100 percent responsible for the quality of your life. You make things happen.
4. **Desire and Discipline: The Dynamic Duo.** This dynamic duo is the key to results every time. Fire them up!
5. **The 4 A's: Awareness, Acknowledge, Assess, Action.** Awareness—recognizing what's happening within you. Acknowledge the areas that need change. Assess what's working and what's not. Take Action with clarity and wisdom.
6. **Pain of Regret or Pain of Discipline.** Choose wisely. Discipline rewards; regret ruins.
7. **JED Is Dead (Justify, Excuse, Defend).** Hear yourself. Stop making excuses and blocking your growth.

Conclusion: Yes, You're Ready

8. **Humor.** Create humor. Laughter, levity, and being light-hearted bring joy and connection.

Chapter 3 Recap: Understanding the Young Brain

We live in a digitally dominated world—unceasing, unrelenting, addicting, and undeniably here to stay. I call this our F.A.S.T. world: one driven by fears, anxiety, stress, and tech. This environment has fostered an epidemic of anxiety, depression, disconnection, loneliness, and stress-related disorders—especially in our youth.

The constant barrage of information and endless stream of online distractions—24/7 news, social media, gaming, videos, texts, and emails—has overwhelmed our children. They're digitally overfed and emotionally undernourished. Since the brain develops based on how it is used, the consequences are clear: technology has ushered in an era of heightened anxiety, distraction, and disconnection, leaving an undeniable impact on mental well-being.

Parents, educating yourself on the effects of excessive screen time is critical. The rising mental unwellness among today's youth is unprecedented. With the teen brain still developing into the late twenties, teaching your children how to build healthy relationships with technology is vital. Mental health professionals advocate for a straightforward yet powerful solution: disconnect. By limiting screen time and reducing dependency on the digital world, we can ease anxiety, break the cycle of addiction, and help lift the veil of depression.

I introduce the "Check Tech" exercise, a powerful tool to help you assess your relationship with technology. You can identify habits that need adjusting by tracking how you spend your time online and reflecting on its emotional impact.

This simple yet eye-opening activity encourages mindfulness and accountability, paving the way for healthier tech boundaries. Remember, leading by example is key—make this a family activity to inspire your kids to develop balanced, intentional relationships with technology.

Chapter 4 Recap: In Family, We Trust

With your foundation reset within yourself, fortified by the Magnificent 8 (M8) and a realistic understanding of how your children's brains operate, Chapter 4 shifts the focus to cultivating trust within your family.

Trust is the glue that holds every healthy relationship together. Without it, everything falls apart. One of the greatest gifts you can offer your children is your unwavering belief in them and trusting that they are more than enough and fully capable of creating a meaningful life on their own. As parents, your trust becomes the super glue reinforcing their confidence with steadfast belief and encouragement. Every child, no matter their age, longs to feel their parents' pride, belief, and trust in them.

When you empower your children with the truth that life is an inside job 9 (M8 #3: If It Is to Be, It Is Up to Me), you teach them to trust themselves—their worth, abilities, ideas, and talents. The goal is to lead by example, showing them that everything they need is already within them. The M8 supports this fundamental truth.

And remember, no one trusts a know-it-all. Stay curious, not judgmental. Be flexible, not rigid. Be kind, not critical.

Chapter 5 Recap: Mindset Shifts for Mastering Your Response + Abilities

Trust isn't given; it's earned and nurtured over time through shared experiences and how you treat one another. There's no finish line for reaching trust. Choosing to behave in a trustworthy manner is a daily decision that shapes your character and the quality of your relationships.

When a family is loving, aligned, and supportive, hearts are full, and the world feels right. But when harmony is disrupted, everyone feels it. Picture your family as a mobile over a crib—each member is an essential piece. If one is off balance or tangled, the entire mobile is affected because all the pieces are intricately connected.

Conclusion: Yes, You're Ready

Applying these Mindset Shifter tools will help you gain a deeper understanding and reframe your perspective, enabling you to lead with care, consistency, and awareness.

Mindset Shifters:

- Go-To Responses Supported by the M8
- Patience + Time
- Kindling Trust
- Teens: Built to Buck
- Behold the Behavior
- The 3 C's: Calm, Clear, and Caring
- Your Behavior Defines Your Leadership
- To Be Understood Is Sublime
- The Parent Traps

Chapter 6 Recap: Tools for Conversations, Connection, and Understanding

This chapter emphasized the importance of balance, family rhythm, deep listening, and open communication—core elements of a family culture built on trust and respect. These tools aren't just about improving parenting skills; they're about creating a home where understanding and thoughtful communication are at the heart of every interaction.

These treasures set the stage for a harmonious and joyful family dynamic, with each tool offering insightful ways to connect with and inspire your kids.

- Know Your Superpowers
- Reasons for Seasons
- Listen, Hear, See, Feel
- Ask Your Children
- Table Talk for Champions
- Blah, blah, blah, Ginger!

Chapter 7 Recap: Be the Muse

This chapter introduces a collection of creative tools designed to transform everyday moments into opportunities for inspiration.

Parents, Grow Up!

Whether through shared hobbies, collaborative projects, or how you navigate daily life, Be the Muse offers a framework for becoming an empowering and influential presence in your children's lives by aligning your actions with your words to inspire respect, spark motivation, and empower meaningful action.

The Muse's Toolbox:

- 10 Wells of Wisdom
- Perpetual Arrival
- The Fantastic 5 Power Tools
- Say It Now, Celebrate Now
- Sage Giants
- Hold On Loosely

Chapter 8 Recap: The Muse Method: Family Activities that Bond and Brighten

This chapter focuses on turning inspiration into action, bringing more vibrancy, connection, and joy into your family life. Through playful and purposeful activities, you've explored ways to deepen relationships, create traditions, and infuse more laughter and harmony into your home.

Each method offers a unique way to connect with your kids, ignite inspiration, and build a culture of respect and joy. These tools help create a treasure trove of memories that your children will carry with them throughout their lives.

The Muse Methods are all about making your family feel seen, loved, and cherished. They are:

- Conversation Jar
- Words of the Week
- Meals Keep It Real
- Family Design
- Let's-Do-It List
- When I Say "I Love You"
- Just-Us Tradition
- Smiles, Giggles, and Awwws

Conclusion: Yes, You're Ready

Chapter 9 Recap: Grab Bag Goodies!

In this final chapter, you were introduced to the motherlode of empowerment: the metaphorical Grab Bag—a collection of life-smart tools packed with reminders, messages, and lessons to keep you grounded, empowered, and present as you navigate life's twists and turns. Life happens every day, and so do you. Why not get skilled at living your best life as your best self?

These tools aren't just for moments of crisis. Their true power lies in regular use, even when life flows smoothly. Consistent practice sharpens your skill, making these tools second nature when the stakes are high. Waiting until you're spiraling to use them often leads to reactive, chaotic decisions—similar to how a novice swimmer tossed into rough waters reacts. The goal? Make your grab bag a constant companion, seamlessly integrated into daily life.

Even better, by using your grab bag, you're teaching and equipping your children to get their own grab bag ready for their ever-evolving lives. The sooner they start practicing with these tools, the sooner they'll experience the self-reliance and confidence that comes from knowing they have what they need to handle life's ups and downs. So, get grabbin'!

Ready! Set! Grab!

Grab Bag Goodies:

- The Magnificent 8 (M8)
- The 5-Fold-Why
- The Yep and Nope of Control
- Equanimity: The Holy Grail
- Be the Otter
- Wishing Your Bed Was Already Made!
- Zip It, Skip It, Flip It!
- Energy Is Everything
- Deliberate Acts of Goodness
- The Happy Sound of Healing
- The Best Way to Tuck Yourself in
- Resilient By Design

Parents, Grow Up!

You did it. You've got this. You're ready. Enjoy the ride.

And, thank you. I hope you find great comfort and confidence in knowing that every tool you need in this book for personal and family transformation lies within these pages—here to support you for a lifetime. From my heart to yours, thank you for valuing my life's purpose and my heart's passion.

I believe in you,

Love, Jill Avery

The ~~End~~ Beginning

It Matters

by Jill Avery

Trust matters.
Words and forgiveness matter.
Kindness and courage matter.
Listening matters.
Tears and laughter matter.
Hugs matter.
Dreams matter.
Character matters.
Presence and patience matter.
To be understood matters.
Memories, gratitude, and mistakes—They all matter.
This is your moment.
Make it matter.
Your family matters.

If you'd like more guidance, motivation, or support—or if you're interested in having me speak to your school, organization, or community—visit www.MyFamilyinFlow.com. I'd be honored to connect to learn more.

As Charlie Mackesy beautifully says in his book, *The Boy, the Mole, the Fox and the Horse*, "The bravest thing you can do is ask for help."[14]

---

[14] Mackesy, Charlie. The Boy, the Mole, the Fox, and the Horse. HarperOne.

Acknowledgments

My God. Did this really happen? Did I actually write a book? It is absolutely true—each of you played a part in making my first book a reality. The journey from thinking *I should write a book* to actually writing one has been monumental. This book encapsulates my whole life—every corner of my mind and heart. Every page holds a piece of who I am, what I believe, and my contribution to strengthening families, teens, and young adults.

Writing this book revealed a layer of vulnerability I hadn't yet met. To write something so personal, knowing it will be released into a world that is both inspiring and cruel, tested my character, self-worth, and lifelong challenge of letting go of control. With people like you in my corner, I have the courage to release control. Terrifying and liberating all at once.

Here's to you—everyone who cheered me on, inspired me, and kept my fire burning bright. My gratitude for you is boundless.

To my readers—thank you for allowing me to be part of your family's journey. What a privilege it is to walk alongside you, and I'm grateful you chose my book to support you. I hope my words empower you in ways that matter most and inspire you to take action: to build the family and life you love and are proud of. I'd love to hear about your progress as your adventure continues.

Parents, Grow Up!

To the incomparable Canyon Ranch staff, I'm deeply grateful to be a part of your ecosystem. Being there always feels like being at home. Each time I depart CR, I feel renewed and whole.

To the Canyon Ranch guests, you are the best audience I could ask for. Your hunger to learn and desire to grow inspires me to do the same.

Arnold Schwarzenegger, I've been inspired by you most of my life. I use your *7 Tools for Life* and share them with my students.

Mel Robbins (@MelRobbins), though we haven't met (yet), you are my Oprah. I make sure my students and parents know about you and the tools you share.

James Clear, your *3-2-1 Thursday* newsletter is a must-have, and I recommend it to everyone I know.

Kristine Carlson (@Kristine_Carlson), your retreats renewed my energy and set my trail ablaze.

Dr. Elizabeth Barrett (@TheReluctantTherapist), thank you for our meaningful conversations on your podcast. You make a difference and create space for others to do the same.

Drasko Raicevic (@PeacefullyAmbitiousCEO), your coaching created unexpected breakthroughs I didn't see coming. I'll never forget those moments.

Lori Young (@OnaMission_Brands), thank you for bringing clarity, direction, and beauty to my brand.

Birgit Spring, you're a gem. Thank you for providing opportunities to reach families through the Saratoga Library.

Anastasia Voll, thank you for helping me pull my mountain of content together—no easy feat.

Jesse Sussman of Book Rocket, you made the audiobook experience AH-MAZING!

Lisa Shiroff, my publisher-turned-friend, you made this process not just rewarding but an absolute joy ride. You're a joy to work with and an even greater joy to know.

Judy Wolthausen and Ann Borgia-Camp, another dynamic duo. Inspiring teachers and extraordinary parents. You've always been "Team Jill," which means more than you know.

Acknowledgments

Dr. Barry Hayes, your guidance has been invaluable.

Nancy Pearne, you are a living angel who always lifts me.

Karen Hyde, if you only knew the breadth and depth of your impact.

To my students—teens and young adults—you are my greatest teachers. You've enriched my soul and filled my life with meaning and awe.

To the parents I coach, your desire and courage to grow as individuals and as parents inspire me daily.

To my powerhouse support squad: Marnie MacMillan-Ruf, Lynne Biddinger, Patty Ballingall Snyder, Julia Bishop, Marla Ryan, Patti Ridenhour, Sandy and Chad Sibilia, Mary Grant Johnson, Faye and Graham Pairman, Stephanie Ingster, Amy Williams, Maria Gress, Susan Hensley, Alyce Parsons, Samantha Talora, Michele Free-Poupart, Carmela Zamora-Robertson, Todd Rafalovich @toddrafalovich, Kenny-Kooker, and Brad Proulx (Pooh Bear). I am damn lucky to call you my tribe.

A special shoutout goes to my sister, Dr. Lisa Morrison—brilliant and precious—who lit the spark with five little words: "You should write a book!"

And to my beautiful and complicated family—my rock(s)—you endured my ups and downs, and I endured your incessant asking, "Are you done yet?" Can you believe it? I can finally say YES! With my heart on these pages and your support behind me, I'm ready to share this book with the world.

Thank you for believing in me.

About the Author

Jill Avery, MA, is a coach, educator, and speaker dedicated to transforming family relationships. With 30 years of experience, Jill has founded multiple businesses focused on empowerment, including the award-winning *All by Myself* series for toddlers, the *Life Launch* program for youth, and *Family in Flow*, designed to help parents build strong, enjoyable relationships with their kids. Known for her warmth, humor, and refreshing approach to family dynamics, Jill is also a featured speaker at Canyon Ranch Wellness Resort.

As a mom of two, she understands the importance of creating strong family foundations. Between coaching sessions, you can find her hiking, jump roping, or enjoying 70s and 80s music with her beloved dog, Lottie. An Ironman athlete and advocate for animals, Jill brings boundless energy, heart, and vitality to everything she does. She lives in the Bay Area with her family.

IG: @jillaveryfamilyinflow
www.MyFamilyinFlow.com

Index

3 C's: Calm, Clear, and Caring	75
5-Fold-Why	132
10 Wells of Wisdom	99
Ask Your Children	92
Be the Otter Visualization	140
Behold the Behavior	73
Big Three Clean-Ups	141
Blah, blah, blah, Ginger!	95
Check Tech	52
Control Chart	135
Conversation Jar	115
Deliberate Acts of Goodness	147
Do-Over Power Tool	104
Energy	144
Equanimity Visualization	138
Expectations Reset	48
Family Attitudes	26
Family Beliefs	25
Family Culture	21
Family Design	119
Family Goals	29
Family Priorities	28
Family Rituals	24
Family Traditions	23
Family Values	23
Fantastic 5 Power Tools	102
F.O.O.T. Power Tool	107
Goodnight Gratitudes	149
Go-To Responses Supported by the M8	66

Parents, Grow Up!

Hold On Loosely	111
Home Environment	27
Humming: The Happy Sound of Healing	148
Just-Us Tradition	123
Kindling Trust	69
Let's-Do-It List	120
Listen, Hear, See, Feel	89
Magnificent 8 #1: Put Your Oxygen Mask on First	33
Magnificent 8 #2: Begin with the End in Mind	34
Magnificent 8 #3: If It Is to Be, It Is Up to Me	34
Magnificent 8 #4: Desire and Discipline: The Dynamic Duo	36
Magnificent 8 #5: The 4 A's	37.
Magnificent 8 #6: Pain of Regret or Pain of Discipline	38
Magnificent 8 #7: JED Is Dead (Justify, Excuse, Defend	39
Magnificent 8 #8: Humor	40
Many Layers of You	171
Meals Keep It Real	118
Natural Rhythms (Reasons for Seasons)	87
Nonnegotiables Power Tool	105
Parenting Leadership	76
Parent Traps: Flattery or Fear	79
Patience + Time	68
Permission Power Tool	104
Perpetual Arrival	101
Photographs for Smiles	124
Pros and Cons Power Tool	103
Resilient Statements	151
Sage Giants	109
Say "I Love You"	121
Say It Now, Celebrate Now	108
Superpowers	85
Table Talk for Champions	93
Teens: Built to Buck	70
Trust questions	59
Understanding	77
Words of the Week	117
Zip It, Skip It, Flip It!	143